T0358495

Careers and Talent Management

Careers and Talent Management challenges and deconstructs the notion of the 'perfect career' in order to provide new perspectives on talent management and career creation. It argues that the skills that organizations typically look for as indicative of superstar performance are not necessarily those that lead to competitive advantage. Attracting and retaining talent is both challenging and complex for organizations, since it is not known, especially at the top level, which employee skills will be most valuable in helping the organization be competitive globally.

In this thoughtful book, Reis bucks the trend on emerging super talents, critically analyzing topics related to the field of general management, careers and talent management – such as leadership, entrepreneurship, gender and diversity – to demonstrate the range of employee skills that can benefit an organization globally. Chapter focuses include global entrepreneurship, remote business practices, and social responsibility.

These new perspectives on talent management will help students of human resource management think critically about the implications of pursuing or encouraging a 'perfect' career trajectory.

Cristina Reis is Associate Professor of Management at the RC Group Research, USA, and has been Visiting Professor and Research Fellow in several European countries. She has several publications in scientific and business journals and is co-editor of *Careers Without Borders*, also published by Routledge.

Careers and Talent Management
A Critical Perspective

Cristina Reis

 Routledge
Taylor & Francis Group

NEW YORK AND LONDON

First published 2016
by Routledge
711 Third Avenue, New York, NY 10017

and by Routledge
2 Park Square, Milton Park, Abingdon, Oxon OX14 4RN

Routledge is an imprint of the Taylor & Francis Group, an informa business

© 2016 Taylor & Francis

British Library Cataloguing in Publication Data
A catalogue record for this book is available from the British Library

Library of Congress Cataloging in Publication Data
A catalog record for this book has been requested

ISBN: 978-0-415-73502-5 (hbk)
ISBN: 978-1-315-81947-1 (ebk)

Typeset in Times New Roman
by Taylor & Francis Books

To those who call me Eagle and remind me of the proverbial saying: 'When a storm is coming, all other birds seek shelter. The Eagle alone, avoids the storm by flying above it.'

Contents

Acknowledgment

I am grateful to the members of the Academy of Management who interacted with me intensively in the past two years and helped me on this project.

Cristina Reis, 2015.

1 A Critical Perspective

Introduction

Critical perspectives, in this book, are a way of using the researcher's clinical eye to analyze societies, organizations and people's social behavior. They are used to discuss what can be improved in certain scientific fields, taking into account the vulnerable people in our societies, and not only to promote the achievement of organizational profit at the cost of the vulnerable. This way of looking at critical perspectives does not negatively affect the issues as usually analyzed in the field of the 'dark side of management', but rather empowers the voice of those who are 'destined' to be victims.

The theoretical framework for a given critical perspective has been described in a previous book, which I co-edited in 2013, entitled *Careers Without Borders*. A summary of what was presented before as a critical perspective now follows, and is adapted to the topics of this book.

The current body of literature in the field of management work continues to lack an exploration of concepts and practices, from a critical perspective, which would address the processes of liberation for organizations, societies and individual lives. A critical perspective of careers and talent management (TM) has some commonalities with the established field of critical management studies regarding the use of critical theories. While critical management studies' analysis tends to focus on labor process analysis (e.g., Braverman, 1974, and Foucault's, 1982, work), critical perspectives, as argued in this book, are open to providing reflections upon the various aspects of organizations, societies and individual lives. The aim is to understand the processes of liberation, not only of the working class, but also of all individuals working for organizations. In other words, while critical management studies concentrate on the processes of liberation within working-class struggles, this critical perspective seeks ways of finding dignified lives for all individuals of all classes.

A given critical perspective does not propose management techniques regarding how to succeed in the business world in this increasingly global society. It is a *reflection* upon how we can be autonomous, because we have the capacity to free ourselves from reliance on various forms of subordination, inequality and various relations of social power. The idea behind this book began with a critical awareness of how careers and TM have been developing, both theoretically and in practice, in organizations – but this is not to say that critical awareness is sufficient for change. It implies a *discussion of how we interconnect with each other and how we are collectively responsible for each other.*

In this book is presented a critique of *different forms of knowledge* and its recognition within the present informal global economy. When the arguments presented are relevant to an analogy, selected ideas from *Utopia*, written by More (1512/1997), will be discussed, since the purpose is to reflect upon how careers and TM have common and to contrast these ideas to those already considered more than four centuries ago.

Useful Ideas from *Utopia*

The island of Utopia '[w]as the ideal commonwealth, painted by More in an ill-disguised philosophical satire on European, and more particularly English, statecraft' More (1997: iii). *Utopia* is a fictional narrative about the manners of a community or society with near-perfect laws. Following *Utopia*, many other authors (e.g., Marx) developed other conceptual utopias and ideal societies.

This book uses ideas from *Utopia* adapted to the contemporary world of organizations and management. Some ideas from *Utopia* were identified as being interesting and as being capable of being related to knowledge management, symbolism, gendered divisions, the usefulness of material and nonmaterial work, and happiness. There follow some examples of citations which may be quoted throughout this book.

Ideas Related to Knowledge Management

In Utopia learning and sharing knowledge seem very simple, and there is no hidden information as in our contemporary, informal global economy.

Despite technology and the internet's expansion, certain forms of knowledge (see Table 1.1 for different forms of knowledge) continue to be in the service of

Table 1.1

A critical perspective	Utopian ways of life
Autonomy	Dependency
Reflection	Assumption
Sees forms of subordination in all classes	Does not see subordination – rather, a perfect social order
Responsibility for one another is challenged, if not a long-term problem	Responsibility for one another is not challenged
Forms of knowledge differentiate individuals	Forms of knowledge are assumed to be shared and understood by all citizens
Dignified ways of living are challenged	Dignity is assumed and not challenged

only a few. Knowledge management did not exist as a concept, but in Utopia they developed ways of information exchange and also managed information.

> Every year twenty of this family come back to the town, after they have stayed two years in the country; and in their room there are another twenty sent from the town, that they may learn country work from those that have been already one year in the country, as they must teach those that come to them the next from the town
>
> More, 1512/1997: 29

Ideas related to symbolism

Utopia was enmeshed in the symbolism of differentiation in labor, inequality and power. However, in Utopia such concepts were not elaborated upon or challenged since Utopians accepted their way of living and social organization. In the next citation, the uniformity of buildings gives an image of social unity and strong walls, and protection from the threats and challenges of the outside world to their way of living.

> The town is compassed with high and thick wall, in which there are many towers and forts ... their buildings are good and are so uniform, that a whole side of a street looks like one house.
>
> More, 1512/1997: 31

Utopians do not challenge whether they are really 'all employed in some useful labour' (37) or whether magistrates distribute their working time and non-working time in a fair way. Although Utopians improve their minds through the time allocated for these activities, 'knowledge' in particular (52) is assumed to be shared and understood by all Utopians.

In Utopia material goods exhibiting scarcity in nature, such as gold and silver, have no exchange value and are culturally perceived as having enhanced superficial value. Only children should be concerned with pearls and gems. If an individual were to wear such materials, they would be regarded as foolish: 'See that great fool that wears pearls and gems, as if he were yet a child' (45).

Ideas Related to Gendered Divisions

Clothes have the function of distinguishing heterosexuality. There is a hierarchical generational order within the family related to business control passed through the male head of the family to other males. Other members of the family serve the superior male hierarchy and other divisions of labor are created among wives, children and the elderly. '[T]hroughout the island they wear the same sort of clothes without any other distinction, except what is necessary to distinguish the two sexes, and the married and unmarried'

(More, 1512: 33); trade generally passes down from father to son and '[w]ives serve their husbands, and children their parents, and always the younger serves the elder' (38).

Ideas Related to Happiness

In Utopia, happiness is achieved through the improvement of its citizens' minds:

> The magistrates never engage the people in unnecessary labour, since the chief to allow the people as much time is necessary for the improvement of their minds, in which they think the happiness of life consists.
>
> More, 1512/1997: 37

While critical theory (e.g., Habermas, 1974) sees the achievement of happiness through reflection, in Utopia it is through the improvement of the mind. However, the difference between the two ideas lies in the belief in individuality and collective ways of thinking. One way is by critical thinking through reflection, where there is a progression to individual autonomy and happiness, while in Utopia it is through the improvement of the mind by collective means of, for example, sharing knowledge. Often, success and satisfaction are mixed with happiness, but the first is more a societal concept rather than an individual concept. Table 1.1 gives some key words that show the differences between a critical perspective and Utopian ways of life.

Talent Management

This section summarizes the different debates on the area of TM. The use of terms such as 'acquisition', 'retention', 'attracting', and 'development of talent' have become common in the field of human resources management, but have scarcely been related to the strategic goals of organizations.

Some authors (e.g., Scullion and Collings, 2011) suggest that TM is concerned with employees who add value to an organization, and that it should be focused on certain employees. The reasoning behind this idea is that it is critical for each organization to establish what talent means to them, since it is connected with their strategic objectives. Therefore, talent requirements vary between organizations.

TM is a growing area derived from five sub-areas. One sub-area (1) is the perspective of standard human resources practices and functions, that is used interchangeably with international human resources management (IHRM) and is a future-oriented perspective of human resources planning, which is about projecting employee/staffing needs; the second sub-area (2) is a focus on the type of individual-level capabilities needed in the future; another sub-area (3) involves the high-performing individuals known as 'high potentials with talent'; sub-area (4) focuses on strategic jobs (or core jobs) that are critical to the organization in terms of creating competitive advantage; the final sub-area

(5) involves the perspective of the capabilities-based approach to strategic human resource management as a subdivision of human resource management.

Two important dimensions have emerged from the perspectives of TM – that of the individual, and that of GTM (global talent management) systems. The following sections summarize the two dimensions.

The Individual Dimension

The individual perspective of TM is often connected with the high levels of current and potential human capital which are adequate for the strategies of multinationals (Tarique and Shuler, 2010) or 'forward-looking companies' (Heidrick and Struggles, 2012). Usually, this perspective focuses on 'superstars' or individuals with high levels of talent (e.g., knowledge, talent and skills), and how these talented people can add value to organizations. In this book, the term 'competency' is frequently used, and in general this means:

> a set of measurable, performance-related characteristics that are critical to driving the organization's strategy goals. A competency should be targeted and behaviorally performance-driven to meet strategic organizational needs. It should be written at a high level and be more general in nature than specific skills, qualifications, or certifications.
>
> (Berger and Berger, 2011)

At the turn of the millennium, popular practitioner studies (Michaels et al., 2001) suggested that the demand for talented employees has exceeded the available supply, forecasting changes in how organizations would have to manage talent shortages. However, they failed to determine which competencies would match the objectives of each organization (e.g., Scullion and Collings, 2011). Today, the trend of talent shortages continues to be discussed, and the 'super-talented' organizational discourse has been converted into a discourse on the emergence of employees who would 'opt out' of organizations and who would transform themselves into independent contractors or individual entrepreneurs (Kofman, 2006; Mackey, Sisodia, and George, 2013). It is a fact that the area of entrepreneurship has grown as an academic discipline in the past decade, with many authors writing on entrepreneurship (e.g., Bates, 2014) as well as the offering of different undergraduate and graduate entrepreneurship programs in many universities.

Are governments hoping that we will all become individualized workers? In the chapter 2, the consequences of an individualized labor market and society will be discussed.

The Global Talent Management Systems Dimension

According to Scullion and Collings (2011), organizations fail to match the supply and demand for talent. However, most large organizations have

IHRM policies and practices implemented systematically to manage employees with high levels of talent. Therefore, most writers in the area of TM started using the wording 'global talent management' (GTM), since it is often connected with international activities.

This dimension seems to suit only those who are considered as having high levels of talent by organizations. Although IHRM activities can be applied to all employees if customized to their needs, it is implied with the notion of TM systems that only those who are selected will have the privilege to be a 'talent'. An example of talent engagement in organizations is executive training programs. Consequently, some consultants (e.g., Heidrick and Struggles) see the emergence of company titles, such as 'Head of Talent', led by employees who will combine global demographic trends and economic crises that seem to be associated with the shortage of talent. Such heads of talent will have a particular agenda aligned with each organization's objectives. Those who are selected as talents may be assigned responsibility and authority in decision-making. A critical perspective reflects upon those who are responsible for others.

Talent Management from a Critical Perspective

A critical perspective challenges the usefulness of the practice of TM for the common good, and not only for organizations. Organizational talents pertain only to certain audiences, and the value and merit of those who have been identified as talents can be challenged outside the organization, particularly if it is a public company which provides services for the common good of all. It is useful to draw an analogy with Utopia here.

In Utopia, talents (or super-performers) do not exist, and even if someone were to propose such an idea, it would run the risk of being regarded as being as enhanced in value and superfluous as jewels are. Jewels are regarded as a resource exhibiting scarcity, but not as fundamental for the common good, and therefore they are superfluous. However, in Utopia, superior hierarchies, such as the magistrates, can distribute what is necessary and unnecessary for the people. In the same way, organizations today may have a head of TM, or corporate executives who are deemed able to identify those who are talented or who will be super-performers, with the belief that those talents will bring competitive advantage to their business (and not necessarily to the common good, as in *Utopia*).

In Utopia, individual differences in knowledge and creativity are not recognized because the common good is prevalent. Working time and non-working time are assigned by magistrates assuming a fair basis of distribution as well as providing the opportunities for the perfect exchange of information and knowledge. Nobody is rewarded for their particular useful contributions. This is in opposition to TM, which aims to differentiate those who super-perform by their competencies and via rewards. A critical perspective would reflect upon dignified ways of working and living rather than individual rewards just to retain talent.

The concept of *TM from a critical perspective* offers a different understanding of the contemporary discursive meaning of TM, whether it be within the individual dimension or the GTM systems dimension. High-performing individuals (known as 'high potentials' or organizational 'superstars') can instead represent a superfluous fantasy in the organizational agenda, since the notion does not include the consequences for the common good. Such an organizational agenda of TM might also propose new forms of subordination, inequality and relations of social power, which a critical perspective challenges.

Authors writing about GTM claim that there are several drivers for the emergence of TM. For example, Scullion and Collings (2011) propose drivers such as globalization, demographics and demand for workers with competencies and motivation, while others concentrate on demographics, work structures and attitudes, and cross-cultural contexts. Practitioner authors (e.g., Boston Consulting Group, 2015) suggest strategies as if they were feasible in the immediate future, such as the strategic workforce planning to select certain future talents. These strategies aim to attract talent from a global labor pool as if all people in the world have equal access to the knowledge required and desired by such organizations.

However, the strategies proposed by most consulting companies for selecting future talents are losing their credibility and trustworthiness. How can companies justify the talents chosen even when they apply measurements of competencies? Most economies, even in the Western world, have IHRM activities which are not practiced or else which are practiced but without transparency (see Reis and Baruch, 2013, for a discussion of the situation in Russia and Portugal). It is possible that the easy access to the internet has made younger generations believe that they can achieve easy money and easy careers. According to Scullion and Collings (2011), the younger generations is less educated, and they suggest there may be a lack of interest in education, as in 'Arab nations where the younger generation sees that connections rather than education are often the route to career success' (23). Other strategies proposed by consulting companies include that of offering different career pathways, yet those who live in the global economy cannot plan because of their uncertainty. The encouragement of careers through virtual work is only for those who have already gained competencies in their fields of endeavor, and such professionals claim that they do not substitute face-to-face meetings as some projects require the establishment of a long-term personal relationship (see the long-term relationship dimension discussed in Baruch and Reis, 2015). Finally, a strategy to attract the elderly, women, etc., is not always feasible since these groups of people are different in terms of their social issues, personal histories, identities and aims.

Talent Development Processes

It is important to describe this process before engaging other topics. It usually includes four broad activities (Garavan, Carbery and Rock, 2012):

identification, design, evaluation and organizational support. These activities can only be developed when the people engaging in this process know the demographics, work structures and cross-cultural contexts, as well as the organizational agenda. Some authors include 'attitudes' in these activities, but since we are in a global and informal economy, attitudes can be more individualistic and therefore they are not so relevant for TM processes. TM processes vary with the objectives of the organization and they deliberately include who to develop, which competencies employees need to develop and the timeframe, tools of performance appraisal, and organizational support from senior management.

In GTM, the development of cross-cultural knowledge (Crossman and Clarke, 2010) is regarded in different ways depending upon the organization and the job required. Some academics believe that cross-cultural knowledge can be gained simply through international projects or research collaborations, or else by working on a project for six months in another country. Others believe that, by living in countries where many ethnicities live together, as in the USA and Brazil, is enough to be acquainted with other cultures and related knowledge. However, this is a misleading idea and experience, since mixed cultural settings will have already developed a new mixed culture.

Cross-cultural concepts vary slightly. For example, some authors use the term cultural intelligence to mean 'the ability to adjust to a variety of cultural environments and circumstances and situations or multicultural situations' (Verghese and D'Netto, 2011); cultural intelligence can be the capability to interact effectively with people from different cultural backgrounds (Thomas and Inkson, 2004). Others focus on 'cultural agility', which is 'the megacompetency which enables professionals to perform successfully in cross-cultural situations' (Caligiuri, 2012). These concepts are often based on the international business field and are not critical. They imply processes of adaptation and do not take into account the strength of the personal identities of the people involved. Other authors suggest business agility, which is the 'ability of a business system to rapidly respond to change by adapting its initial stable configuration' (Wieland and Wallenburg, 2012), but this is no different from actors in a theater and is not an experience a genuine life.' Another concept more aligned with critical perspectives is that of *cross-cultural competence*, which is 'the ability to understand people from different cultures and engage with them effectively' (Rasmussen and Sieck, 2015).

Another important point in GTM is the literature on expatriate management. This suggests that there is a shortage of managers with the necessary competencies and experiences to work effectively across cultures (Collings, Scullion and Morley, 2007). Tarique and Shuler (2012) recommend the engagement of employees early in their careers in international experiences and developmental programs, such as the practice of 'talent flow' which can be considered a TM process. According to Carr, Inkson and Thorn (2005), talent flow is a process whereby economically valuable individuals migrate between countries, and this process is related to the choice of engaging in a boundaryless global career (see Baruch and Reis, 2015 for the conditions that apply to the creation of a global and boundaryless career).

Another talent development process is the transfer of tacit and valuable knowledge. 'Tacit knowledge' might be described as informal unwritten knowledge. This concept is important to the theoretical framework of this book as well as when the analysis integrates the critical perspective together with the Utopian way of life. Is tacit knowledge as valuable as it is in *Utopia*?

According to Goffin and Koners (2011), the effective transfer of tacit knowledge generally requires extensive personal contact, regular interaction and trust. This kind of knowledge can only be revealed through practice in a particular context and is transmitted through social networks (Schmidt and Hunter, 1993). To some extent, it is 'captured' when the knowledge holder joins a network or a community of practice. In this sense, this form of knowledge is similar to what we know to be the way of life in Utopia but which is considered a reality in our present societies.

Organizational tacit knowledge is often found in organizations at the senior management level or among specialists (Calo, 2008). Often, those who possess tacit knowledge are not aware of it or how valuable it can be to others. For example, Reis (2004) coined the term 'unspoken work', namely work that has not been elaborated into words and thoughts but which is practiced in daily routines at work and which is often intruded with personal life. Such unspoken work is valuable tacit knowledge.

Other TM processes include the development of leaders. Stahl et al. (2007) found that organizations would develop an outline of competencies that their leaders require, and employees were evaluated within such charters. On the positive side, different charters were used for different categories of employees and talents.

The process is also used to retain talent (Barron, 2004; Berta, 2006; Brandemuehl, 2009; Kirkland, 2007), since it is regarded by the employee as an investment from part of the organization. Some authors argue that organizations with limited resources are forced to target certain exclusive leaders who will benefit from these programs (Brandemuehl, 2009; Caligiuri and Tarique, 2009) since not all employees benefit from experience development programs. How can organizations know who to develop according to these charters? It is by assessing those individuals with individual personality traits (Caligiuri and Tarique, 2009). Tarique and Shuler (2012), based on the assumption that not everyone benefits equally from developmental experiences, argue that these learners may only benefit if they are predisposed to develop their skills in the first place (see also Caligiuri, 2000).

Critical perspectives would certainly challenge and reflect upon this procedure of TM. How can practitioners develop transparency about individual personality traits when we know that people can develop different forms of identities? If certain individual personality traits are considered as core for organizations, how can individuals gain those desirable traits and how are individuals differentiated by age, gender, ethnicity, class, background, qualifications, etc.?

Other practices related to TM processes include the development of succession planning. Organizations without succession planning are more likely to experience loss of talent (Cohn, Khurana and Reeves, 2005). Succession and replacement planning (Rothwell, 2001) is a short-term practice generated to identify individuals who can fill core jobs in emergencies.

The experiential leadership training or development provided to these chosen people by such organizations implies the design of specific competencies and tools of performance appraisal aligned with the organizational objectives proposed by senior management. In the same way, global leadership talent aims to have the right leadership competencies. Conceptual models have been elaborated (e.g., Sloan, Hazucha and Van Katwyk, 2003) in this respect that include clarifying the organizational globalization strategy, defining global leadership roles and requirements, and designing TM systems.

Another TM practice is retaining talent; this involves all those activities that are required to prevent those considered to be talented employees from leaving the organization. Needless to say that those employees who have job satisfaction and higher levels of performance are less likely to leave an organization (e.g., Lockwood, 2007). Some strategies include career development, training and repatriation.

Career development should exist in all organizations and can provide ideas about career planning to all employees and not only to emergent leaders. Employees who have an understanding of their career paths are reassured that their organizations value their efforts and are less likely to leave. Training provides specific skills, such as communicating with certain audiences, which most employees assume is easy in practice yet are surprised when their messages are not heard. Repatriation can be facilitated by organizational practices when expatriates return to their home country or to headquarters. If the employee is strongly supported by the organization in returning home, the organization will offer mentoring programs and career planning sessions to retain the expatriate (Lazarova and Caliguiri, 2001).

The Structure and Content of the Book

This book includes seven chapters on the topic of careers and TM from a critical perspective, and each of the chapters discuss a self-contained topic. I am grateful to the seven international reviewers of the proposal for this book, who gave me the motivation to write each chapter. In general, they all noted that the innovation of the book is to be found in its new perspectives on careers and TM discourses at a time when social and economic changes are highly volatile.

Chapter 1 explains the meaning of a 'critical perspective' and the reason for presenting analogies with *Utopia*. All the chapters have a section with comments made from a critical perspective and concerning *Utopia*. Chapter 2 is the longest chapter, and explains the changes in the nature of work in the new economy, TM research and practitioner agendas, and new careers, and questions whether they are useful among other related contemporaneous topics. Chapter 3 presents a review of careers without borders with an emphasis on a TM perspective. Although there has been discussion that there are few opportunities for careers and talents, this chapter presents a reflection upon the global economy and suggests solutions; for example, governments need to increase the number of talented experts who are able to respect other relations of social power and know how to put in practice development projects (see Reis, 2016). Chapter 4 examines those leaders in society who are somehow considered talent managers in light of a theoretical framework of the analysis of Carl Rogers and Lacan. Chapter 5 concerns how global entrepreneurs deal with business remotely, and presents an example of a useful career in entrepreneurship. Chapter 6 is probably the most controversial chapter because it discusses how the work produced by families is used by organizations; in particular, the family work produced for those in the highest management positions. Finally, Chapter 7 presents a theoretical framework for how senior executives can have a socially responsible and boundaryless career, which draws a balanced conclusion on the topic raised in the first chapter.

References

Barron, T. (2004) The link between leadership development retention, *T+D*, 58(4), 58–65.

Baruch, Y. & Reis, C. (2015) How global are boundaryless careers and how boundaryless are global careers? Challenges and a theoretical perspective, *Thunderbird International Business Review*. http://dx.doi.org/10.1002/tie.21712

Bates, M. E. (2014) *The Reluctant Entrepreneurs: Making a Living Doing What You Love*, Colorado: Niwot Press.

Berger, L. & Berger, D. (2011) *The Talent Management Handbook: Creating a Sustainable Competitive Advantage by Selecting, Developing and Promoting the Best People*, New York: McGraw-Hill.

Berta, D. (2006) Leadership development bolsters employee retention, *Nation's Restaurant News*, 40(37), 18.

Boston Consulting Group (2015) Leadership & Talent. Retrieved 1 October 2015, from www.bcgperspectives.com/talent_and_leadership

Brandemuehl, J. (2009) Talent reviews and succession planning matter more during tough economic times, *T+D*, 63(6), 17.

Braverman, H. (1974) *Labor and Monopoly Capital: The Degradation of Work in the Twentieth Century*. London: Monthly Review Press.

Caligiuri, P. M. (2000) The big five personality characteristics as predictors of expatriate's desire to terminate the assignment and supervisor-rated performance, *Personnel Psychology, 53*(1), 67–88.

Caligiuri, P. (2012) *Cultural Agility: Building a Pipeline of Successful Global Professionals*. San Francisco, CA: Jossey-Bass.

Caligiuri, P. & Tarique, I. (2009) Predicting effectiveness in global leadership activities, *Journal World of Business*, 44(3), 336–346.

Caligiuri, P. M. & Dragoni, L. (2014) Global leadership development. In D. G. Collings, G. T. Wood and P. M. Caligiuri, *The Routledge Companion to International Human Resource Management*, London and New York: Routledge. 226–239.

Calo, T. J. (2008) Talent management in the ear of the aging workforce: the critical role of knowledge transfer, *Public Personnel Management*, 37(4), 403–416.

Carr, S. C., Inkson, K. & Thorn, K. (2005) From global careers to talent flow: reinterpreting 'brain drain', *Journal of World Business*, 40(4), 386–398.

Cohn, J. M., Khurana, R. & Reeves, L. (2005) Growing talent as if your business depended on it, *Harvard Business Review*, 83, 62–70.

Collings, D. G., Scullion, H. & Morley, M. J. (2007) Changing patterns of global staffing in the multinational enterprise: challenges to the conventional expatriate assignment and emerging alternatives, *Journal of World of Business*, 42(2), 198.

Crossman, J. E. & Clarke, M. (2010) International experience and graduate employability: stakeholder perceptions on the connection, *Higher Education: The International Journal of Higher Education and Educational Planning*, 59(5), 599–613.

Garavan, T. N., Carbery, R. & Rock, A. (2012) Mapping talent development: definition, scope and architecture, *European Journal of Training and Development*, 36(1), 5–24.

Goffin, K. & Koners, U. (2011) Tacit knowledge, lessons learnt, and new product development, *Journal of Product Innovation Management*, 28, 300–318.

Foucault, M. (1982) The subject and power, *Critical Inquiry*, 8(4), 777–795.

Habermas, J. (1974) *Theory and Practice* (J. Viertal, Trans.). London: Heinemann.

Heidrick & Struggles (2012) Board of Directors Survey. Retrieved 1 October 2015, from   www.heidrick.com/~/media/Publications%20and%20Reports/WCD_2012 BoardSurvey.pdf

Kirkland, S. (2007) If you build it, they will stay: leadership development in the American Cancer Society, *Organizations Development Journal*, 25(2), 77–80.

Kofman, F. (2006) *Conscious Business: How to Build Value Through Values*. Boulder, CO: Sounds True Inc.

Lazarova, M. & Caliguiri, P. (2001) Retaining repatriates: the role of organizational support practices, *Journal of World of Business*, 36(4), 389.

Lockwood, N. R. (2007) Leveraging employee engagement for competitive advantage, *Society for Human Resource Management Research Quarterly*, 1, 1–12.

Mackey, J., Sisodia, R. & George, B.(2013) *Conscious Capitalism: Liberating the Heroic Spirit of Business*, Boston, Mass: Harvard Business School Corporation.

Michaels, E., Handfield-Jones, H. & Axelrod, B. (2001) *War for Talent*. Boston, MA: Harvard Business School Press Books.

More, T. (1512/1997) *Utopia*. Mineola, NY: Dover Publications.

Rasmussen, L. & Sieck, W. (2015) Culture-general competence: evidence from a cognitive field study of professionals who work in many cultures, *International Journal of Intercultural Relations*, 48, 75–90.

Reis, C. (2004) *Men Working as Managers in a European Multinational Company*, München: Rainer Hampp Verlag.

Reis, C. (2016) Managers' remote work and expertise across cultures in small–medium companies, *Journal of Applied Management and Entrepreneurship* (in press).

Scullion, H. and Collings, D. (Eds.) (2011) *Global Talent Management*. London: Routledge.

Rothwell, W. J. (2001) *Effective Succession Planning: Ensuring Leadership Continuity and Building Talent from Within*. NY: AMACOM.

Schmidt, F. L. & Hunter, J. E. (1993) Tacit knowledge, practical intelligence, general mental ability, and job knowledge, *Current Directions in Psychological Science*, 2(1), 8–9.

Sloan, E. B., Hazucha, J. F., Van Katwyk, P. T. (2003) Strategic management of global leadership talent. In W. Mobley, M. Li & Y. Wang, *Advances in Global Leadership*. Bingley: Emerald. 235–274.

Stahl, G. K., Bjorkman, I., Farndale, E., Morris, S. S., Stiles, P., Trevor, J. & Wright, P. M. (2007) Global Talent Management: How Leading Multinationals Build and Sustain Their Talent Pipeline. Faculty and Research Working Paper, Fontainebleau, France: INSEAD.

Tarique, I. & Shuler, R. S. (2010) Global talent management: literature review, integrative framework, and suggestions for future research, *Journal of World Business*, 45(2), 122–133.

Tarique, I. & Schuler, R. S. (2012) Global talent management: theoretical perspectives, systems, and challenges. In G. Stahl, I. Björkman & S. Morris. *Handbook of Research in International Human Resource Management*. Cheltenham, UK: Edward Elgar. 205–219.

Thomas, D. C. & Inkson, K. (2004) *Cultural Intelligence: Living and Working Globally*. San Francisco: Berrett Koehler Publishers, Inc.

Verghese, T. & D'Netto, B. (2011) Cultural intelligence and openness: essential elements of effective global leadership, *International Review of Business Research Papers*, 7(1), 191–200.

Wieland, A. & Marcus Wallenburg, C. (2012) Dealing with supply chain risks, *International Journal of Physical Distribution & Logistics Management*, 42(10), 887–905.

2 Useful Careers

Introduction

Theoretically, there are different concepts and types of careers which researchers in the field of careers and TM discuss. We live in a dynamic labor market, and researchers now claim that we no longer have linear careers or hierarchical progressions, and that we instead have non-traditional careers. What has engendered these changes in careers? The nature of the work and the effects of a globalized economy. All these changes have engendered changes in education as well as some confusing concepts in TM and careers theory. In this chapter, we reflect upon the usefulness of non-traditional careers changes.

The nature of work changes

The focus on the nature of work changes has concentrated on teamwork and leadership. For example, Schein (1996) suggested that both general management functions, such as co-ordination and integration, and individual management skills, such as analytical, inter-personal and emotional competence, will become more important as work becomes more technically complex, requiring greater co-ordination and integration at lower and lower levels within the hierarchies of organizations. The expectation is that 'everyone will be expected to become somewhat competent at management and leadership' (Schein, 1996: 84).

Other changes include processes of individualization. In the past decade, some authors (e.g., Beck, 1992, and Beck and Beck-Gernsheim, 1995) have noticed radical trends in the labor market in Western societies as freeing agents from traditional structures and as being at the origins of fundamental transformations of relationships between people. Others (e.g., Beck, Giddens and Lash, 1994) hold another perspective and have noted the significance of knowledge-intensive production, which relies on rapid innovation. Lash identified 'reflexive economies', where people no longer use traditional work structures (e.g., organizations now have flatter hierarchies). In a reflexive economy, people are individualized but at the same time they need to communicate and cooperate intensively and use rules and resources in a flexible way.

Obviously, Lash's work has been criticized since this theory excludes most people from the labor market. The basis of the individualization of employees in reflexive economies demands highly skilled workers with the right skills and opportunities to survive in such economies. This type of individualized reflexive economy, where innovation is continuous, may be somewhat oppressive rather than liberating.

Employees need to invest more time in their careers to obtain results, they need to update their knowledge and skills to perform new tasks, which change frequently, and they need to exhibit continuous and greater concentration to understand how their business is integrated in the global economy, and most likely they need to travel frequently. Consequently, some researchers query whether there is a decline in talent in organizations (McDonnell, 2011). However, this trend is more oppressive than the reality, and saying that talent is in decline is to misdiagnose a deep problem in the globalized economy, which works only for highly skilled and privileged individuals.

This is not to say that we will return to old structures which no longer bring innovation, but certainly we need to re-think changes to values such as loyalty and commitment to work and relationships. Loyalty and commitment disappear in oppressive economies, and people are lost in seeking personalized coaching to fit into what is perceived as the present reality in the job market.

In Utopia, there is an established order and people are loyal and committed to their work and relationships. Everything works to perfection in Utopia, but the individualized reflexive global economy that we live in today is also 'Utopian' and socially unrealistic. While Utopia might be an example of an extreme society and economy with inflexible structures, our present economy – with too many flexible structures – is also disastrous. In other words, we are now 'forced' to do whatever we want, but we cannot afford it.

We were 'forced' to believe that work–life balance is a new and great opportunity for all kinds of careers. Many people, after a certain age, are made redundant without any pre-retirement preparation. Again, we have been 'forced' to believe that they are unproductive failures, when in reality the new globalized economy has been a fiasco and has not created innovative jobs for now-redundant productive people. We have also been 'forced' to believe that everybody can be an entrepreneur or an independent contractor. Many people who want to become entrepreneurs have plenty of ideas but they do not manage them in practice for reasons which range from the right opportunities to skills and health. Again, they become individual victims in an economy where not everyone can be an entrepreneur.

The emergence of TM has been a consequence of these economic changes and it raises many questions – the answers to which are not transparent. How do organizations develop ideal talents? Can we all be talents? Have we gone back to some sort of Utopian social and economic order? Who are the talents that organizations choose for executive positions?

The Effects of Globalization

Organizations have changed to drive off the competition deriving from the effects of globalization. Many countries, mainly from the Far East, have started offering products and services at lower cost compared to the Western world and, consequently, organizations have started to make lay-offs and have moved towards flatter organizational structures.

Western countries have outsourced production to China, information technology (IT) to India, and other services, potentially, to anywhere for routine jobs. This has resulted in high competitiveness and fewer jobs for people in Western countries. Another outcome is that for managers to make career progress they have to move organizations more often, as well as having to move horizontally within organizations.

Therefore, managing one's own career development may also include sophisticated movement between several other work organizations and new networks of professionals. The effects of globalization have brought more than what could be regarded as mere challenges to people's means of earning a living. Most Western careerists have lived in societies led by organizations which have responded to a patriarchal order of structuring, or where employees' careers have been taken care of, or else somehow designed or created, mainly within large organizations.

As argued in the previous section, the conceptualization of individualization in a reflexive economy (Beck, Giddens and Lash, 1994)) is a representation of a socio-cultural image which marginalizes most people – it underestimates new forms of subordination and inequality affecting most people's work and relationships. As a consequence, in the past decade, new career concepts have been developed while social and organizational changes have been portrayed as something revolutionary that can bring equal opportunities for everybody. However, these new careers seem to have more problems than challenges (Baruch and Vardi, 2015). Are we all able to engage in these new forms of careers? Are these useful careers?

New Forms of Careers

A new important theoretical form of career that emerged in the 1990s was that of the 'boundaryless career', regarded as a 'tapestry' or as an inter-firm concept which 'constitutes the threads that bind people and firms, and, in turn, broader industrial and economic activities' (Arthur and Rousseau, 1996: 12). Today, the boundaryless career (where all boundaries disappear) is an idea rather than a reality (Inkson et al., 2012). It is an overstatement, and people cannot live and work wherever they want (see Reis and Baruch, 2013; Baruch and Reis, 2015). People move because of loss of employment or by necessity rather than by engaging in boundaryless careers by choice.

Managing one's own career brings more uncertainty, at the individual level, about developing realistic opportunities for well-paid work. In such a context, people no longer compete for posts in organizations, as before, but instead search for opportunities within temporary contracts or portfolios (sometimes taking more than one assignment at the same time). In order to arrive at an opportunity to earn money, the individual may be confronted with higher competition and must dedicate increasing the hours dedicated to such new career demands. In the past, organizations took care of their employees, but with the new forms of careers, they have been strongly criticized for their patriarchal meritocratic systems. Employees previously experienced less ambiguity and seemed to generate more personal wealth; they also had less freedom and were less individualized. Today organizations are concerned with their employees' performances but they fail to see how an insecure employee will not perform as desired.

Now that we are in charge of our own careers, we have less stability and are probably overstressed. The way in which new careers are portrayed is that we may have the freedom to grow at our own pace and make our own choices, which appeals to some people, but it is problematic for most of us and is problematic in our societies.

In addition, the intensification of paid work decreases the amount of time individuals are able to devote to their leisure time, occupational changes and – of course – all of that which belongs to our private lives. Some have supported the view that managing one's own career development requires the individual growth of:

> personal abilities, skills, and competencies, such as a sense of self-direction and self-reliance, the ability to think through issues traditionally resolved by management, as well as the ability to connect on one's own with co-workers in order to solve problems and get the right things done.
>
> (Walker, 1996: 265)

However, this view is related to diversity management and restricts the understanding of managing one's own career development. The view of individual growth is useless when the basis of developing certain abilities, skills and competencies seems to be filtered by such answers.

The *intelligent career* is another new form of career and works well only in knowledge-based economies. It consists of know-why/who/whom dimensions (see Baruch and Reis, 2015), and not many people live in an active labor market or else experience the conditions to access the three dimensions of this form of career. For example, the dimension 'who' of the intelligent career, which consists of the useful access to networks, is not for everybody in every profession.

In addition to the dimensions of the intelligent career, there is the surge of TM, which tends to manage certain selected individual career profiles (e.g., managers with certain skills, potentialities, performance levels and capabilities) and aims, at the same time, to have a certain level of influence and control in certain types of labor market. On the basis of these 'ideal' selected career profiles, organizations and independent agencies construct portfolios of individuals, and trade people's careers as 'products' to different work organizations. Subsequently, if managers' and talent managers' consultants (who deal with organizations) are in control of certain labor markets, they are also in control of individuals' career development through admitting or excluding people. The intelligent career may only have a minor role if the market is controlled in such ways.

Another type of new career is the *protean career* (e.g., Hall, 1976; Hall and Mirvis, 1996; Schein, 1993), but type of career is problematic when the person has no desire or inclination to change occupation. The concept derives from the Greek god Proteus, who could change himself according to his will, and the concept has been applied to those new careers where people can change according to their will and to careers they choose. However, the protean career's concept works for certain positions in management but not for every profession or all workers. For example, medical doctors invest in their studies over several years and a change in their careers and lives is not always possible. The protean career maybe a good management technique when employees are not performing, particularly for those in the highest organizational hierarchy although, but such employees are still protected by their pensions. The application of these concepts to every occupation has been disastrous, with severe consequences for the wealth and health of people and societies.

The labor market is constantly changing and the conceptual trend is towards organizational anorexia or leaner management, which will eventually collapse because it is socially unsustainable. The consequences are that these changes create instability in people's lives and in society. It is very difficult to get a new job when you reach a certain age. Many workers have no pension and are forced to work until late in life to gain money to survive. People can be fired easily but cannot always start a second career. These changes are not useful for a sustainable society or useful careers.

Some people can enjoy a career late in life, but they need to be dynamic and they do not necessarily need to change occupation. This is the case of the *post-corporate career* (Peiperl and Baruch, 1997), which usually results as a consequence of a forced retirement (often called 'voluntary retirement') from a previous job. It brings a sense of loss of certainty, confidence and stability.

Another new career type is the *multidirectional career* (Kucht and Lackstrom, 1986), although it usually ends in just one direction. There is also the new career type called the *resilience career* (Coutu, 2002), a concept which assumes that we need to survive professional rejection and, consequently, that we need to be resilient. For example, many academics are required to publish in journals with 99 percent rejection rates. The acceptance of an article in these journals is managed by people who belong to an informal club/alliance and an article may take a long time to be recognized or accepted. Some academics never achieve the 'reward' of having a publication in such journals.

Another new career is the *kaleidoscope career* (Sullivan and Mainiero, 2008), which is considered to be authentic, with balance and exciting challenges. However, not everybody can take career breaks or part-time jobs, since most have fixed expenses to pay such as mortgages, children or dependents, etc. All these careers concepts try to glorify such new careers, but they are either problematic or unrealistic.

Academic Publishing: A New Pesilience Career or Not Useful?

In the arena of academic publishing there are several confusing ideas currently being discussed among academics all over the world. Recently, in some European countries, and abruptly, governments have required that both public and private universities should produce research centers. These research centers would be evaluated by international committees concerning the research they produce and would benefit from being financed by the government, but researchers should not be monetarily rewarded. For example, in Portugal most professors in private universities are paid by the hour and suddenly they were required to attend long meetings and produce high-quality research without being paid. High-quality research publications are those rated on, for example, Elsevier's Scopus.

This is even more awkward since some public and private universities did not have researchers prepared to publish in such journals and they could not write fluently in English. More intriguing is that many Portuguese universities had their own publishing press and, for generations, their professors published in the publishing presses of their universities. This is still the case for many other universities around the world, including some Ivy League universities in the USA with good public relations (PR) systems. They still produce books from their own facilities, in which they seem to cite most of the research of their faculty authors. They are producing new, fresh research on their own, even if much of what they write about has been written before in other journals, *but they have their own perspectives.* If most universities were to adopt this system, it is likely that things would become fairer and less like a business.

This old solution is probably still the best available for academic publishing since they write for a specific audience and the faculty receives little (or almost no) money from the big business that is international publishing. In addition, most faculties are not honored by their institutions for publishing books or journal articles that are rated highly in those international lists of scientific journals. Therefore, there are many urgent changes to be made in the academic publishing business which need to be reflected and acted upon for the sake of the prestige of the academic profession.

There is no doubt that academics lose prestige and character, unless they work for such groups as the Ivy League where they seem to be more protected. ***There are ten reasons why academics are losing respect for their professions.*** *(This list is only an example, and a very lengthy list could be constructed. In addition, see point 10 for differences with other professions.)*

1 There are many lists of ranking scientific journals; elaborated by country and by institutions.

2 Besides the rankings of these scientific journals in these international lists, there are other ways in which certain academics are trying to get noticed, namely by counting the high number of citations that their research has generated. This 'ability' is manifested through internet search engines (e.g., Google, Research Gate and others). Apparently, it is useful to cite yourself frequently and everywhere if the editor of the journal allows it. However, traditional and influential scientists know that the best research is not the most cited, because it often requires long-term preparation to understand what is written.

3 The process of reviewing an article is lengthy. If the authors respect academic publishing ethics, they can only send an article to one journal. The overall process can take between three and six months and, if after reviewing and resubmission the article is rejected, which happens frequently, the authors usually send it to another journal. In general, the estimated time until final acceptance in a highly ranked journal is around two years. (This is not to say that some academics do not get their articles published right away.)

4 Reviewers, as authors, are not paid for their scientific publications because this is considered a service to the profession. Sometimes, reviewers are honored by having their names in the journal as reviewers. However, many institutions do not appraise service as a reviewer, and faculties thus feel that they are not honored.

5 Ranked publications assume such high importance because they are a business, both for publishers and in terms of bringing money to universities' research centers. Some faculty may receive an individual research grant, the money of which is usually used in their research and not on themselves.

6 Most academics dedicate their lifetime to the profession and have no leisure time or money to enjoy other things in life. The loss of respect for an academic career is related to their loyalty to their institutions (e.g. see Sennett, 1998), colleagues, friends and other traditional values seem to vanish into depression. There are no longer highly respected professors upon whom one might rely for mentorship.

7 Those who have conversations with academics find that many academics come from poor backgrounds and unprivileged upbringings. It has become particularly insulting for academics that universities allow con-sulting firms to introduce changes and allow 'consultants' to say, for example: 'if you were the son or daughter of a McDonalds franchise owner, you wouldn't work here anyway!' Academics listen to such irritating comments and do not respond to such cruel insults, probably because they are too polite or they think that this cannot be real.

8 Losing academic character is a TM issue because publishing in highly rated scientific journals and receiving numerous citations constitute an

ability that is required to get a good job. While football players are well-remunerated in their sport – or rather in the entertainment industry – academics seem to have lost their character and to have forgotten to demand their monetary rewards. Academic service and writing is well-earned and should be highly remunerated because of the risks academics take in publishing.

9 Unfortunately, some academics receive their opportunity to access power through teaching, where some engage in sexual discrimination and harassment; through reviewing other research work anonymously, which they think allows them to insult people; through evaluating other faculties where the sexual discrimination and harassment happens again. I have observed in more than one country the male faculty giving final grades to female students while they look at their bodies. One male faculty member showed me an assignment which was failed and then called the female student concerned to his office – she ended up with a 'B' because she was good looking. The faculty member expressed this without any concern and he will probably continue with the same methodology for grading students. Sexual harassment is more complex because it is a long-term process whereby the person in a position of power diminishes the work and the capabilities of the student (or the other faculty being evaluated). The aim is to explore the fragile side of those victims until they get to the point of asking either sexual favors (for review see O'Leary-Kelly et al., 2009) or else derive pleasure from watching the victim destroyed and depressed. The victim might also be a male student who does not display strong signs of masculinity or a male junior faculty member. Sexual harassment by women also happens, although it is uncommon.

10 Academics are no different from others in the corporate world, entrepreneurs or people in other occupations (e.g., the police). However, as educators and researchers they are in a leading position whereby they should display exemplary conduct in society. Therefore, the faculty should be awarded for such efforts and be well-remunerated, both by business publishers and their institutions. Since this is not happening via institutions and businesses, there are smaller efforts rewarding academics from organizations, such as the Academy of Management, among others.

Reflection upon New Forms of Careers

There is a need to reflect upon the problems of the new forms of careers for individuals as well as the usefulness of TM practices in organizations.

The new forms of careers, from a critical perspective, do not free up individuals' life choices as portrayed in most theories. TM can be a useful tool for organizations because it justifies the tasks of talent acquisition and retention. However, individuals classified as high-potential performers or 'superstars' are often part of company political agenda and do not always perform well in the public eye (e.g., the CEOs of ENRON and other organizations).

Changes such as the restructuring of the labor market and downsizing, and its problems, are manifested in employment rates, career paths, personal health, family well-being and financial safety. In the old economy, people were considered to be followers of imposed structures with many communication barriers. The transformation of the labor market involves conducting new precarious psychological contracts in many globalized economies rather than new prosperous contract inventions. We are all knowledge workers – we produce knowledge but we are not able to stop lean management, particularly in the most fragile economies, thereby allowing people to become vulnerable to all kinds of illicit work and trade in order to access 'money'.

All career theories have major issues and there are no leading theories. For example, career capital theory is an adaptation of human capital theory, and most concepts and ideas are unrealistic (see Baruch and Reis, 2015).

There are *changes in education* that aim to produce practical careers which mean, for most labor market analysts, a way of having people employed in unsatisfactory ways and in precarious work. Most people do not have the same quality of life that their parents had. The trend has been to produce professionalized people rather than critical thinkers or people following their vocation. Many universities have, on their websites, different types of discourses where they state that they teach critical thinking to their students. However, these discourses are often translated into feelings and short stories. They do not teach how to build an independent idea supported by research which may produce a useful conceptual contribution. Concepts, rather than feelings and opinions, can become actions and ways of life as well as the destiny of many learners.

Most practical professionalized people are not interested in concepts but in being. There are several tools available to demonstrate such ways of living (e.g., Facebook or other social media tools). These social media tools support the dreams of those interested in being and will rarely interact by doing something for society or organizations through a valuable contribution. This is obviously a choice, and those who have the values to make a contribution are generally a rarity in present-day societies.

Professionalized degrees include Chartered Professional Accountants (CPAs) and all other kinds of professional certifications. These are models for practical people, but they do not develop ways of reflecting upon the sources of organizational and social problems. Many universities produce incubators for entrepreneurship and teamwork. They produce practical jobs with a high risk of failure because not everybody can be an entrepreneur. They produce a surplus of certified people in the labor market rather than useful careers and talents which might be sustainable in the future.

Another example has been the significant production of MBAs without any specific vocational direction. It is assumed that they learn to manage 'something' or people, but they do not have credibility in the labor market and they still do not have stability. Most MBA students become consultants, sometimes hired by the same company where they had been hired for their first job before they gained their MBAs. These companies, instead of having MBAs as employees, buy their services. These MBAs still have to manage their own careers as consultants, which often results in a quite limited and insecure career. These are not useful careers because such career models do not fit the circumstances of all people.

Talent Management Research Agenda

There are two perspectives on TM which are active in organizations and Western societies: (1) the discourses on, and unclear practices of, TM conducted by businesses and consulting firms; (2) the lack of theoretical frameworks for this academic field.

Al Ariss et al. (2014) state that research is 'lagging behind business in offering vision and leadership in this field' (173) and they offer a review of key theoretical concepts and practices. The reasons are that TM is often used as a term in HR practice and is used in succession-planning practices. The controversy relies upon whether TM is about all employees or only highly talented employees or high-potential employees. Another major controversy noticed by the authors is the failure of organizations in the recruitment process, 'despite the care taken to recruit that talent' (173), and that these processes vary by country.

There is also a lack of trust in the recruitment process and measurements of TM performance, and this perception undermines TM.

According to Al Ariss et al. (2014), 'many multinational enterprises have adopted TM strategies, with medium- and small-sized companies being less involved' (174). They summarized the work of Stahl et al. (2012), who studied 33 multinational corporations with headquarters in 18 countries. Stahl et al. found two main understandings of TM: an approach limited to high-potential employees, labeled 'differentiated'; and an inclusive approach which is available to all employees. However, the main conclusion was that these corporations align their TM practices with their strategies and values, which becomes a unique process for each corporation. For global corporations, the authors deciphered six principles: (1) alignment with strategy, (2) internal consistency, (3) cultural involvement, (4) managing involvement, (5) a balance of global and local needs, and (6) employer branding through differentiation. Another practice used by global corporations is expatriation, which raises other controversial issues, mainly in that repatriation processes are not always successful for corporations who have lost individuals to other corporations.

In summary, there is no agreement as to the concept of 'talent' in business (Al Ariss, 2014) because there are many TM practices and perspectives on how the most talented of employees can make best use of their knowledge and experiences to become a sustainable foundation of competitive advantage for corporations. Employees need to be rewarded and selected, and if they perceive that they are not progressing in their work or firm, the risk is that they will lose creativity and become dissatisfied with their work and careers. In Utopia, talented people do not exist, just as precious stones have no value and are used as toys for children or fools. Like talents, precious stones are recognized as rare but not needed. In our globalized economy, firms lead by competitive advantage economic practices and need to retain their talents. It becomes problematic for individuals if they move from one organization to another, since each firm has different TM processes connected with their strategy and values.

Therefore, career theories should be an important platform supporting the practices and concepts of TM. The field of careers lacks considerable development and is stuck with the 'new careers' in a world where many authors and migrants believe that boundaryless careers are possible and easy to engage in and progress. Baruch and Reis (2015) proposed a theoretical framework questioning whether global careers can be boundaryless, and vice-versa, concluding this is a possibility with several limitations, being only possible for some people, with certain conditions, and for certain cultures. TM strategies reflect fantasies, and the field of careers needs to go beyond what has been written regarding 'new careers' to support new and transparent concepts and practices in TM.

Scandals in TM abound in corporations (e.g., the managers of ENRON in the USA, the British Petroleum (BP) managers involved in the Gulf Coast scandal) where young managers are promoted and awarded as the best managers despite only a few basic qualifications and a total lack of social experience. It is a mystery how these CEOs achieved such a high-level positions.

The exploitation of people continues to be severe wherever there is a lack of political control of practices which favor only some investors and not employees. For example, as of 2015, the UK has many qualified people working 'zero-hours contracts', meaning that people have no benefits or rights such as maternity or paternity leave, etc. Although the law in the UK says that after one month of work in a company, employers have to issue a contract with all basic benefits and rights, this is not the case in practice and there is no control on the part of government authorities'(BBC news, 2015). The same situation exists in other European countries and in several sectors. It is quite striking that academics, i.e., highly educated people, are accepting these contracts when the law says that, after 1–6 months, depending upon the country, they can get a permanent contract with benefits. Many academics, after 10 years of working for the same private university, are still signing temporary contracts (zero-hours contracts) and do not complain to government authorities. It is possible that some academics have tried to change their circumstances for the good of all but without success. The reasons for such a lack of success can vary, from an inability to find a lawyer interested in the cause, to a lack of money or a fear of losing work, etc.

On one occasion, in the USA, one lawyer asked me for the reason why academics tend to be unhappy people. I was surprised by the question, but years later I thought about it and I think that it is important to point out some features shared with the business world. In the same way as business people seek sucess in the business world, people in search of the glory of an academic career can display obsessive and detached behavior and relationships. In this context Pahl (1995), particularly referring to businessmen, describes the neurotic behavior of those who, in their obsession with work and 'the search for glory', exhibit consistent patterns of long working hours, few holidays and detachment from home life. Grey (1994) suggests that non-work lives can become totally subordinate to the notion of career, as 'friends become transformed into "contacts" and social activity becomes "networking"' (492), as individuals have illusions of professional progress. However, most rewards in the academic world are nonmonetary and unsatisfactory when compared to the business world's average remuneration. In the field of GTM, Farndale et al. (2014) demonstrate a largely financially driven balancing act related to any type of expatriation (i.e., global work opportunity). It is possible that academics with big or delusional egos are prone to more frustration because their rewards in search of glory comprise honors only recognized among small groups of people. An academic's unhappiness can be driven by the demands of unpaid, hard work which requires a lifetime of dedication and isolation.

Is this a useful career? There is no question that we need people who conduct research and who teach, but *this is just one example among many types of careers that need to be reviewed*, not only at the psychological and contractual level but also in recognizing talents. Universities are not managing their internal talents or capitalizing on talents for strategic success (Joyce and Slocum, 2012). Psychology-contract theory suggests that employee perceptions of the extent to which talent quality are rewarded are not being applied to academic careers in most institutions (Höglund, 2012: 126). Moreover, we can observe in private universities many unqualified people or quasi-academics dedicated to becoming politicians, who are claiming similar rewards and honors as dedicated full-time academics. This has resulted in the decline of the value of this occupation as well as personal frustrations and lack of esteem.

The development of a differentiated pool of employees can contribute to the recognition of careers and the well-being of people in society. Distinct from Utopia, where nobody is differentiated or rewarded differently, critical perspectives want to empower the voices of those who are discriminated against and who are the victims of non-transparent practices. Critical perspectives propose that merit should be rewarded in different ways, and at the same time that it should not create significant gaps in wealth and well-being in societies.

However, most TM concepts continue to focus only on the competitive advantage of organizations, with distorted discourses on the investment in people's performance, recruitment and retention. In Chapter 3, I will try to link these discourses to different contexts and countries.

Future Research on Useful Careers

Today, we have several management tools designed to measure the performance of employees who are talented (see Berger and Berger, 2010). These tools were developed to show transparency in recruitment practices and to retain people in organizations. However, the use of these tools is being challenged by the new research agenda. Nevertheless, it is questionable whether these tools are being used in practice or in adequate ways because, as discussed, each corporation adapts its own processes of TM and each corporation has a unique strategy and values. It may be worth reviewing the laws regarding the transparency of each corporation's strategy and values before applying any given TM process. TM processes should support equal opportunities in recruitment, promotion and retention in the labor market.

Recruitment through Skype Interviews

Those who have been trying to get a job, or those who are practitioners of recruitment, know that these practices are not always fair or else are discriminatory. Another book containing hilarious situations and the scripts of Skype interviews designed *to identify talents* could easily be written (obviously respecting the privacy of the people and institutions involved).

Several organizations are now inviting candidates to engage in Skype or telephone interviews, which are relatively cheap methods of recruitment. Usually, several candidates are invited for these interviews on the same day and institutions end up mixing-up names and the positions for which the candidate has applied. This process of recruiting people through Skype or by telephone is undignified for everyone and, in addition, there is a great deal of disturbance in the communication process (see Chapter 5 for remote communication pitfalls). Remote interview techniques mean that organizations do not have to pay for the candidate's transportation, food, etc., in order to meet them in a face-to-face interview, and as such the investment in time and money is conveniently significantly reduced. It is also easier to justify the preference for a certain candidate through this method because the information given to the outside world is easy to manipulate and hide. These are bad practices of recruitment and, if candidates believe in best practice, *they should refuse to give a preliminary interview by telephone or Skype or other similar forms of technology*. These practices of using such technologies have merely increased the problems of discrimination in recruitment which already existed (e.g., preferences for the 'old boy network', etc.).

Good organizations will not accept Skype or telephone interviews, and candidates should not accept these forms of being interviewed even when they are desperate for a job. If an organization invests money in recruitment, it means that it is taking the candidate seriously, which dignifies both the individual and the organization. This does not mean that such investment avoids discrimination, but with costlier procedures of recruitment organizations are more careful. Research in this area is promising, because it can uncover new forms of bad recruitment practices and might provide ways of achieving transparency for future generations.

Online Teaching and Electronic Mentoring

Online teaching is a controversial method of teaching and the debate has grown in recent years with the rise of low-cost internet facilities. The individual controversy concerns the difference between an online experience and an in-person experience. The institutional controversy is between most Universities reducing faculty-associated expenses and other elite schools who can provide the excitement of a face-to-face educational process.

Many universities are under pressure from accreditation boards, and the coursework they offer prepares students for specific professions (e.g., chartered accountants or other required skills) as these fulfil the working-class dream of having a job immediately. College education has long been about a classroom with a professor and sufficient students to interact (between 5 and 30 students) to explore a range of perspectives on a difficult topic, which creates an excitement and chemistry in the classroom that cannot be replicated online. While some elite institutions are maintaining such classes with their key instructors, they are at the same time engaging on massive online open courses (MOOCs).

For big universities, in many countries, larger lectures had the assistance of graduate students (teaching assistants) who could lead less-challenging or well-elaborated discussions and graded papers. Sometimes, massive classes are split among several teaching assistants who will grade multiple-choice tests and provide discussion boards with standard replies and a lot of debate. However, this is not the same as having an interaction with a professor/scientist who has the knowledge to monitor different perspectives. Those manual and textbook publishers and universities who do not value such high-profile professors/ scientists are now trying to develop software programs to teach classes and computer-grade essays.

These approaches have attained such a level of absurdity that there are teaching models now being used on campus, such as the 'flipped classroom', where instructors prepare the material needed as homework and use classroom time for peer and interactive learning. Other teaching class models use practitioners and consultants and are video-recorded to replace instructors in the future.

Another interesting argument against online courses is that higher education is an experience, and not only about learning a subject. It includes the experience of socializing with smart people and sitting in inspiring historical places, that most people will never access, as users of that space. Nowadays, many people attend courses on a part-time basis, trying to balance their coursework with family demands or with the requirements of full-time jobs.

The excitement of sitting in a classroom should be similar to attending a Broadway show in person (which is not the same as watching one on TV at home). Professors are able to speak enthusiastically just as actors/actresses do and, if able to do so, they can elaborate using humor and jokes to receive full classrooms and laughs. Live, monitored discussions and interactions constitute a show led by a professor/scientist with the knowledge and ability to create excitement, which allows for innovation through the discovery of new perspectives and the elaboration of genuine creativity.

My suggestion is that online courses will have success with the best students, but there is another possibility, namely a combination of face-to-face courses and Skype courses. This is very different from online teaching. It also follows the same concluding suggestion from the famous article of Heller (2013) on MOOCs (or Laptop U). This methodology works well when students already know the professor/scientist style of teaching and have had face-to-face interaction for one to two months with him/her. Skype classes should only be provided following this experience, and students still have to come to the classroom. The Skype method is easy to use but requires at least two screens: one where the professor speaks and watches the classroom (e.g., through a laptop) and another screen where the course material (such as course slides) is presented. The assistance of a student (who volunteers to help with the slides) to explain any issue which was not clear through electronic communication to the classroom is crucial in this process. Usually, students respect the professor/scientist because they know him/her from previous face-to-face classes, and my first-hand experience with this method has seen it work very well. The advantage is mainly for the professor, because he/she can go to an important scientific conference, thereby enriching the discussion in the classroom environment, or else can be physically present in other classrooms in other countries. This is a very convenient method for universities with subsidiaries in other countries, or those with international exchange programs, and it is certainly financial advantageous.

Mentoring employees should be a personal and face-to-face process and not electronic. Although many authors advocate that much is being said in social media and note that people say things they would never disclose in a face-to-face meeting, many misunderstandings take place in social media/electronic meetings. The same point is valid for students who are sometimes victims of misbehavior by other students, colleagues or the faculty. Electronic mentoring can be dysfunctional because physical signs (e.g., being tired) can be hidden behind a video camera. Institutions should engage in face-to-face high-quality connections (Dutton and Heaphy, 2003) and provide clear procedures and training as to how students can be mentored. However, some companies avoid face-to-face mentoring processes because not being present in the same room with employees, they avoid the company of discriminatory practices. In these companies, mentoring is a voluntary and informal process whereby the mentor usually proposes a process of self-discovery for each individual. It reflects an individual choice which is not monitored electronically regarding the advantages and disadvantages of the process.

Online Social Media Networks

Nowadays, social media networks (e.g., Facebook, LinkedIn, etc.) are used by many people, and some interesting observations have been made which deserve a note of caution, particularly those regarding practices of TM. Again, this is not a comprehensive list and only comprises some observations. There are people who invite others to be a part of their professional and social networks and who are accepted even when they do not know who the people in question are. One of my contacts was linking with three or four professionals from the public sector every day. Sometimes, they were even adding dead people to their network. What is the aim of this practice?

Well, apparently, there is nothing wrong with this practice because those engaging in it seem to amuse themselves, at least until one discovers that this is being practiced by professionals in leading positions in multinationals and the government, etc. It is even more astonishing when these leaders check on others' friends/professionals networks without asking permission of the owner of the network. Are our networks for ourselves or for transactions by other people? Why do they engage in such 'unapproved spying' on others networks?

I decided to observe this phenomenon with a friend who had a well-known family business in the USA but who is now retired. We entered my first professional network and, afterwards, his professional network connected to mine. My friend had only three people on his network contacts and had no photograph, but we found out that both my male and female contacts were spying on him (and only on him and nobody else from my other contacts). Were they looking for my 'famous' friend's sponsorship for their projects?

My friend and I also noticed that several women who worked as 'talent managers' for well-known multinationals (including a famous brand of lingerie) were trying to approach him by spying. My friend was never contacted directly by email or any other means by these female managers, and one wonders what these women of different ages, all working in HR, were trying to achieve when searching for my friend and by leaving their profiles on his LinkedIn page. This shows disrespect for serious people working in HR and TM.

I left these social networks forever and returned to the time of postal cards and personal email to keep in touch, and updated only with my real friends and serious professional endorsements (if needed).

Discourses on the Shortage of Talented Employees

Another topic for future research in strategic HRM/TM, particularly regarding GTM, is whether there really is a shortage of talented employees. Obviously, there will not be a shortage if you give people opportunities to develop their skills (including ethical and social background) and willingness to perform. Corporations expect to find people ready-made to fit their strategies and values without any long-term investment in human resources development. They are opening-up a platform for a lack of transparency and discourses which mainly derive from practitioners who can only see the immediate (or what they can see and smell right in front of them) and who cannot conceptualize other ways of resolving their needs within best practices. I should remind the reader, here, of the Portuguese prince, the *Infante de Sagres*, who draw a map to India for oceanic navigators (e.g., Vasco da Gama) without ever going there in practice. Most people would need to experience such a sea route ten times or more before they could draw a map or anything about it. TM strategic best practices are often difficult to understand for most practitioners if they have no academic background in fields such as careers and talent management and therefore intensive training is necessary for most practitioners in order to control the use of discriminatory discourses.

Conclusion

This chapter discussed how the nature of work changes, new careers and their effects, and TM agendas, and it included emergent new topics related to TM. For example, the topic on changes in education about promoting entrepreneurship as a way of creating employment for all is also a discourse of distortion which does not produce useful careers. As discussed, not everybody is likely to be successful as an entrepreneur. Political trends in education are to produce professionalized or practical people, which can cause a surplus in the labor market. Future research could examine the career progress and paths of individuals who have attained wealth. This is more than merely writing their biographies – it is about analyzing their lives and careers using methodologies which uncover what is unsaid or 'unspoken' (see Reis, 2004; Reis, 2014) in people's lives.

References

Al Ariss, A., Cascio, W. F. & Jaap, P. (2014) Talent management: current theories and future research directions, *Journal of World Business*, 49, 173–179.

Arthur, M. B. & Rousseau, D. M. (1996) *The Boundaryless Career: A New Employment Principle for a New Organizational Era*. Oxford: Oxford University Press.

BBC News (2015) Q&A: What are zero-hours contracts? Retrieved 1 October 2015, from www.bbc.com/news/business-23573442

Beck, U. (1992) *Risk Society: Towards a New Modernity*. London, Thousand Oaks, New Delhi: Sage Publications.

Beck, U. & Beck-Gernsheim, E. (1995) *The Normal Chaos of Love*. Cambridge: Polity Press.

Beck, U., Giddens, A. & Lash, S. (1994) *Reflexive Modernization*. Stanford, CA: Stanford University Press.

Baruch, Y. & Reis, C. (2015) How global are boundaryless careers and how boundaryless are global careers? Challenges and a theoretical perspective, *Thunderbird International Business Review*. http://dx.doi.org/10.1002/tie.21712

Baruch, Y. & Vardi, Y. (2015) A fresh look at the dark side of contemporary careers: toward a realistic discourse. *British Journal of Management*. http://dx.doi.org/10.1111/1467-8551.12107

Berger, L. & Dorothy Berger, D. (2010) *The Talent Management Handbook: Creating a Sustainable Competitive Advantage by Selecting, Developing, and Promoting the Best People.* USA: McGraw Hill Books.

Coutu, D. (2002) How Resilience Works, *Harvard Business Review*, 80(5), 46–50.

Dutton, J. E. & Heaphy, E. D. (2003) The Power of High-Quality Connections. In K. Cameron, J. E. Dutton, & R. E. Quinn, *Positive Organizational Scholarship.* San Francisco, CA: Berrett-Koehler Publishers, 263–278.

Farndale, E., Pai, A., Sparrow, P. & Scullion, H. (2014) Balancing individual and organizational goals in global talent management: a mutual-benefits perspective, *Journal World of Business*, 49, 204–214.

Grey, C. (1994) Career as a project of the self and labour process discipline, *Sociology*, 28(2), 479–497.

Hall, D. T. (1976) *Careers in Organizations*, Pacific Palisades, CA: Goodyear Pub. Co.

Hall, D. T. & Mirvis, P. H. (1996) The new protean career: psychological success and the path with a heart. In D. T. Hall *et al.*, *The Career is Dead – Long Live the Career: A Relational Approach to Careers.* San Francisco, CA: Jossey-Bass Publishers. 15–45.

Heller, N. (2013) Laptop U: Has the future of college moved online?, *Annals of Higher Education, The New Yorker*, 89(14), 80–91.

Höglund, M. (2012) Quid pro quo? Examining talent management through the lens of psychological contracts, *Personnel Review*, 41(2), 126–142.

Inkson, K., Gunz, H., Ganesh, S. & Roper, J. (2012) Boundaryless careers: bringing back boundaries, *Organization Studies*, 33, 323–340.

Joyce, W. F. & Slocum, J. W. (2012) Top management talent, strategic capabilities, and firm performance, *Organizational Dynamics*, 41(3), 183–193.

Kucht, W. G. & Lackstrom, W. C. (1986), Multi-directional career pathing, *Employment Relations Today*, 13, 75–79.

McDonnell, A. (2011) Still fighting the war for talent? Bridging the science versus practice gap, *Journal of Business and Psychology*, 26(2), 169–173.

Mirvis, P. H. & Hall, D. T. (1996) Psychological success and the boundaryless career. In M. B. Arthur & D. M. Rousseau (1996) *The Boundaryless Career: A New Employment Principle for a New Organizational Era.* Oxford: Oxford University Press. 237–255.

O'Leary-Kelly, A. M., Bowes-Sperry, L., Bates, C. A. & Lean, E. R. (2009) Sexual harassment at work: a decade (plus) of progress. *Journal of Management*, 35(3), 503–536.

Pahl, R. (1995) *After Success: Fin-de-Siécle Anxiety and Identity*, Cambridge: Polity Press.

Peiperl, M. & Baruch, Y. (1997) Back to square zero: the post-corporate career, *Organizational Dynamics*, Spring, 7–22.

Reis, C. (2004) *Men Working as Managers in a European Multinational Company*, München; Mering: Rainer Hampp Verlag.

Reis, C. (2014) Listening to the material life in discursive practices, *Tamara Journal for Critical Organizational Inquire*, 12(2) 1–6.

Reis, C. & Baruch, Y. (Eds.) (2013) *Careers without Borders: Critical Perspectives*, New York: Routledge.

Schein, E. H. (1993) How can organizations learn faster? The challenge of entering the green room, *Sloan Management Review*, 34(2), 85–92.

Schein, E. (1996) Developments in the 21st century, *The Academy of Management Executive*, X(4), 80–88.

Sennett, R. (1998) *The Corrosion of Character*, New York: W.W. Norton & Company.

Sloan, E. B., Hazucha, J. F., Van Katwyk, P. T. (2003) Strategic management of global leadership talent. In W. Mobley, M. Li & Y. Wang, *Advances in Global Leadership*. Bingley: Emerald. 235–274.

Stahl, G., Bjorkman, I., Farndale, E., Morris, S., Paauwe, J. & Stiles, P. (2012) Six principles of effective global talent management, *MIT Sloan Management Review*, 53(2), 25–32.

Sullivan, S. E. & Mainiero, L. (2008) Using the kaleidoscope career model to understand the changing patterns of women's careers: designing HRD programs that attract and retain women, *Advances in Developing Human Resources*, 10(1), 32–49.

Walker, B. A. (1996) The value of diversity in career self-development in Hall *et al.* (Eds.), *The Career is Dead – Long Live the Career: A Relational Approach to Careers*, San Francisco: Jossey-Bass Publishers.

3 Identifying Talents Cross-Culturally

Introduction

This chapter begins with a review of careers in several countries by Reis and Baruch (2013), and includes the TM agenda (in particular regarding views on the topic of talent identification cross-culturally). I would like to point out that this review is not representative of the authors' views of their studies but rather is an interpretation of the author of this book in light of TM as it is practiced today. The inclusion of the countries discussed depended upon the availability of the researchers for the previous book, Reis and Baruch (2013), and the experiences of the author of the present book, who has lived and worked in different countries.

Al Ariss et al. (2014) state that they

> envision that TM programs need to move beyond the performance-based discourse traditionally found in organizations if they are to generate positive impacts on society as a whole and address the linkages among the different levels and contexts (177).

These contexts are defined in key levels, such as the individual, organizational, institutional and national/international sectors, and it is at the national and contextual levels that TM respects its context and the 'recognition of how TM practices can transcend (or not) national borders among different industries, networks, and organizations' (177).

Another important issue for TM with regards to similar changes to those we saw for new careers in Chapter 2 is the freedom that individuals will have to manage their own careers. Al Ariss et al. (2014) see changes in TM and employees at the global level. Employees are available globally and for so long as they have the required knowledge. Of course, this view has a major counterpoint, which is *how employees gain such freedom and the required specific knowledge to succeed in a global economy independently of organizations.*

Farndale et al. (2014) argue that *psychological contract theory* will change and that *there is a need to understand the new reciprocities between organizations and people.* If there are 'perceived promises being made, [this] shows the value of building and [an] "inside-out" approach, i.e., an internally driven GTM strategy' (213).

In the next section, this chapter will point out, country by country, changes in TM. For example, it will consider whether *employees are gaining the freedom and knowledge* to succeed in a global economy independently of organizations, as well as whether there are any positive or negative changes in the *psychological contract.*

Careers and Talent Management without Borders

The studies of each country derive from Reis and Baruch (2013) and they follow a model of clustering countries based on attitudinal dimensions as proposed by Ronen and Shenkar (1985). In this chapter, the countries follow an order guided either by geographical proximity or else by career and TM issues that require urgent attention. I begin with the USA because this book is first being published in that country.

The USA and Canada

The *USA* study on careers emphasized concerns with the experiences of marginalized groups, such as undocumented immigrants, which are not well reported. TM can do very little for an illegal worker, since they have been placed at the mercy of unscrupulous employers, mainly because of their illegal status. This is highly political, but obviously there is a need for urgent change and 'there appears to be a need to place a higher emphasis on diversity management' (Al Ariss et al., 2014).

Regarding TM agendas in the USA, there is an emphasis in *the identification of superstars and talents which seems to concentrate on the sports and entertainment industries.* Other individuals who are superstars are usually *executives* of large organizations. Usually, these individuals have studied at Ivy League universities or universities with large endowments. Sometimes, these endowments are from people who do not know what to do with their money. This can be a vicious circle, because many of these donors do not know anything about research in these universities and simply follow the famous name and tradition of such institutions in the USA by thinking that they are making a contribution to their society. Surprisingly, institutions do not always excel in their research, and donors should investigate further whether such generous investments should go to other, smaller institutions.

Canada continues to be regarded as a young country intersected by colonialist immigration policies, influenced by the people, policies and the media of the USA. Although Canada made efforts in the 1980s to advance with an identity based on multiculturalism (which was supposed to be unique to Canada), this idea vanished for lack of political and financial investment. In recent decades, Canada has given unplanned access to several waves of refugees and immigrants.

Regarding TM in Canada, employees do not seem to have gained any freedom or to have new and better psychological contracts. Most available jobs are not well paid and require specific professional knowledge (as such for those chartered accountants and marketing specialists rather than global strategists). It has a large, traditional, unhappy working class which is dependent upon its organizations, and most of its refugees and new immigrants survive in low-paid jobs or professionalized, noncreative jobs.

Europe

Western Europe

The *UK* study claims that many people are marginalized in their work, with particular emphasis on low-skilled tasks being performed by people with higher-level degrees. There is evidence that talent is being misused, with no signs of any changes in this sense. Therefore, people are not gaining freedom as expected, and rather they are taking more than one job (mostly low skilled or professionalized) and are working under precarious psychological contracts in order to have a decent life. In the previous chapter, 'zero-hours contracts' were discussed as having a negative impact on people's social, health and financial well-being; however, since it empowers and makes new entrepreneurs rich, this continues to be a trend (not well explained and seriously discussed in the academic field of entrepreneurship).

The UK does not have a significant tradition of university endowments as in the USA, but the British do have social class issues in their minds and they isolate themselves from 'the rest'. The question 'where do you live in this town?' divides people right away, at the very first moment that they meet and talk. The UK has one of the oldest democracies, but this does not mean that everyone is integrated in the same way if they are not from certain social circles and wealth categories. 'The rest' will hardly be identified as talents or potential candidates for a good job if they are outside of such a social system.

Regarding education, European countries have long had issues of prejudice preventing the recognition of international qualifications, in particular those deriving from countries outside the EU. However, it is still not easy to have a foreign degree deriving from the USA or Canada recognized in the EU because of national-based protectionism, although the Bologna agreement achieved some uniformity with three educational cycles (Bachelor's, Master's and PhD). However, the traditional PhD in the UK required worldwide originality and it was difficult to gain such degree. The British Library claimed to have all credible worldwide publications and could check all kinds of information in this regard. Some British universities started substituting PhDs and MPhils (a degree similar to the German doctorate before the Habilitation thesis) with speedier doctorates termed DBAs. These degrees have less academic or scientific rigor and fit the political requirements of satisfying the statistics regarding numbers of highly qualified people for the EU's headquarters in Brussels.

Are academics being fabricated in European countries by certain 'international academic elites' while the marginalized workers (sometimes with higher-level qualifications from the UK) continue to produce low-skilled work for the sake of their own survival and for an economy that does not care about people/humanity? It is most likely that, with the new wave of refugees deriving mainly from North Africa (and Africa in general), the Middle East and other countries, this situation in the labor market and education will remain unchanged. TM in the UK seems to exist only for certain socially protected circles (disregarding the education, degrees or skills one may have).

The *Austrian* study found, remarkably, that there is very little written about Austrian citizens who work for international organizations in Vienna. No reasons were given for this finding, but one might be tempted to wonder whether those employees are protected talents. The study also had strong concerns regarding the attitudes and political position of immigrants. Austrians have had discussions about immigrants' movements (or people who live near their geographical borders to work in Austria) for years, but there are no empirical data or studies about their immigrants' lives and career goals.

Regarding TM, Austria has a culture where people believe in equal opportunities for everyone. It is possible that their talents tend to work in Vienna for international organizations or else for their neighbors in Germany and Switzerland, which have stronger or more stable global economies. If Austria receives lower-skilled workers from other neighboring countries (see Hungary), they also protect and export talents. Having said that, they have no concerns about retaining their own talents, whether they be executives, academics or others.

The study from *Portugal* focused on the polarization of social classes between the few very rich business owners and the majority of the 'remediados' who are nearly poor or else poor by EU standards. In the past decade, the country has been transformed into a country for tourists. Tourism is interesting, but if it is not carefully watched in relation to the management of HR, it becomes a pool for the exploitation of national employees (few Western European immigrants and refugees have a preference to be positioned as workers in Portugal). The few executives or family business owners who do relatively well manage their business at the cost of people with precarious contracts. Although Portugal has highly skilled workers in most industries, in the past decade many professionals have chosen to migrate to other countries.

There is knowledge about TM, and many consultants are teaching creative concepts in this area. However, such practices do not seem to have continuity within the national reality. Most family-owned companies (including multinationals operating in Portugal) do not take human resource management practices seriously, and this holds even more for anything which relates to TM.

There are governmental agencies in place to investigate illegal contracts and implement penalties (including international auditors from the EU), but little seems to get resolved until someone hires a skillful lawyer at his/her own expense. They may resolve the situation for one person, but the same situation continues for other employees. For example, academics who work for private universities have been signing six-month contracts (or zero-hours contracts, which are paid by the hour with no benefits) for 10-year periods. In principle, the law says that academics should be employed permanently after six months if they continue to work at the same institution. This situation has been ignored, both by academics for fear of losing work in the area in which they are professionalized, and – mysteriously – by government agencies. In the previous chapter, this phenomenon was also acknowledged in the UK and, in the same way, without results.

Psychological contracts changed negatively to the extend people are regarded as 'things' by their bosses and uncomfortable in doing any kind of work. Other extreme situations aggravate poverty in Portugal, such as the abrupt and excessive taxation of private property and services. Many were obliged to sell their property for small sums of money to be free of tax debts to other opportunistic people who had cash. Only those who innovated and transformed their property into a profitable business (which in a small country is very difficult) have a better life.

As in other countries, most people do not seem to have sufficient knowledge to gain freedom from organizations or to succeed in the global economy, particularly when unforeseen changes happen locally in laws and in relation to taxation which only benefit few people (there are few politicians and entrepreneurs in specific sectors, mainly tourism, who benefited from such changes at work).

The Nordic Countries

The study from *Sweden* was very original in expressing the physical and emotional stress caused by extensive traveling required for work. Regarding TM, the study discusses managerially invasive rules in relation to employee well-being. If this is the case, psychological contracts will have a negative impact on employees because they increase tension between employers and employees. They did not seem to reach a consensus as to what is desired in a global economy.

Sweden is recognized as being among those rich countries in the global economy where employees could gain the freedom and the required specific knowledge to be independent of organizations. However, this is not the case for the majority of the Swedish, and it is probably not even desirable. Future research could investigate whether there is a desire to become free from being a salaried employee.

Finland was not included in the book of Reis and Baruch (2013), but I did some research on multinationals in the country. Regarding TM – and surprisingly – Finland is still regarded as a Swedish colony, whereby young elites learn in universities who accept only those who speak native Swedish. While there are Finnish–Swedish elites who are probably in the queue to become talents and who have access to good jobs, there remain immigrants from African countries who clean apartments, offices and other spaces. These jobs are also given to Finnish graduates who have not immediately accessed good employment. Such cleaning jobs were identified by politicians as green because the conditions of their social status changed, since young people are taking them and now they have green detergents or other utensils with green brands. However, I witnessed in the building in which I rented my apartment (which was in downtown Helsinki) cleaners who could not speak a word of Finnish, Swedish or even English. These marginalized people do not exist for Finnish people, who cannot even admit that they are there right in front of their own eyes. They defend a discourse of transparency and a minimalist life without domestic helpers even though they have marginalized people working for them. I tried to investigate the statistics for the numbers of cleaners but no institution seemed to know anything about it. There were other forms of hiding marginalized work which I also bumped into it. People with small companies hired private services with the label 'consultants' to help with domestic tasks. Such a country that is famous for its transparency and minimalist lifestyle was nothing but a country with a new discourse transformed into the fabricated higher status of new innovation and transparency.

In Finland, the new psychological contracts were fabricated discourses which were causing unhappiness among young Finnish people who contended with what they could get at that moment. Although the Finnish claim to have greater knowledge in almost everything, nobody I interviewed who worked for a multinational saw their way out of being free from institutions.

Eastern Countries

The *Hungary* study presented a large wave of immigration to Western countries. At the same time, they also experienced the re-entry of Hungarian citizens from neighboring Eastern European countries or else workers who commuted between Hungary and neighboring countries.

Immigration tolerance was a concern, with particular emphasis on Hungarian citizens who return to their own home country from other Eastern European countries. Taking into account such social and economic changes in Hungary, HR and TM practices may only exist at the academic level.

The *Russian* study claims that there is a lack of importance attached to HRM practices, resulting in its low investment. There is no basic knowledge, mostly due to the fact that HRM practices were Western and did not fit with Soviet ideology and education. Most private companies are owned and managed by their founders, who demand obedience from family members and do not see the necessity in learning Western business practices. Young people feel discriminated against, and opt out to go abroad for their education and to initiate their careers in Western countries. In opposition, there are young people who 'somehow' are integrated in the Russian labor market system and are enjoying careers with rapid promotion opportunities.

Eastern countries, as in emerging economies such as India, China and Russia, may need to link TM to their business practices to leverage existing talent (McDonnell et al., 2012).

The Border between Europe and the Middle East

The study from *Turkey* is not concerned with immigration or the country's young people because the economy is growing. However, Turkey is one of the biggest exporters of students to the USA, and one wonders what they do to their own immigrants, refugees and marginalized people arriving every day from North Africa and the Middle East. It also seems that they have high ratios of women in politics and in the administration of higher education. However, such jobs are not powerful – as in other countries – and are disadvantaged in other large business organizations where money and power are concentrated. Turkey is probably one of the most interesting countries to investigate because it is on the border of Europe and the Middle East. It receives financial support from both global regions and it plays a crucial role as the global guardian of their frontiers.

Regarding TM, Turkey is even more interesting because it has knowledge and excellent researchers in the field of social responsibility, but in practice they are low profile and it has an 'uncertain and unknown' economy. It is a country with a mysterious and gendered labor market, and most people are definitely not independent of organizations (except for those male entrepreneurs who dominate in terms of money and power).

South America

The study from *Brazil* claims that immigrants have been encouraged by political and social elites in sending particular communities from Brazil to other countries. As the economy has improved over the past decade, many Brazilians have returned to their home country. However, in the last two years Brazil has again been facing socio-economic challenges based on alleged corruption by political elites and social classes' economic differences (which is different from facing ethnicity-related bias, as is the case for those from Spanish-speaking countries).

TM in Brazil is discussed among academics and other informed people, but it is not sufficient for changes in terms of knowledge and independence from organizations. Regarding psychological contracts, employees continue to obey the traditional order of submission between master and subject.

Argentina seems to be a somewhat an undefined place to emigrate to because there is no difference between being a local or a foreigner. Most Argentineans in leading positions belong to the second or third generation of immigrants, and even newcomers are regarded as Argentinians without differentiation. These elites seem to be in a position to enjoy freedom from organizations if they become owners of property. However, those in non-leading positions may have psychological contracts of subjugation to elites and property owners.

New Zealand and Australia

The study from *New Zealand* and *Australia* focused on the importance of geographical isolation, with many young people trying to engage in careers. The study claims that HRM for Australians and New Zealanders follows Western practices, which was often made possible due to the efforts of those who may not think of themselves as pursuing careers. It seems that there is an elite class of people with careers who are potential candidates to become talents and others who do not even notice that there are these possibilities. Nevertheless, there is a challenge in terms of transparent information and knowledge for access to equal opportunities.

The Far East and Asia

The study from *China* is very interesting because there is an increase in foreign investment in their country while at the same time leading positions are being given to foreigners. The local Chinese population continues to be marginalized in terms of TM.

The study from *Japan* presents foreign employees facing multiple barriers to Japanese socialization. At the same time, Japanese employees feel under-appreciated and take up a passive role, assuming that there is slow change in their organizations. There are strong barriers to TM in Japanese organizations, although it may be practiced by foreign employees who work for foreign organizations in Japan.

India highlighted the importance of technology, because they are a country of offshore industries (mainly IT). There is a young, talented population taking IT jobs with the expectation of quick promotion and which has caused a high degree of job rotation. Those who do not engage in these new careers are either independent entrepreneurs or else marginalized in ways that are unthinkable in Western countries.

Waves of Refugees and Immigrants to Western Countries and Wealthier Economies

Form this review, we might notice there are elites and marginalized people in every country. However, regarding TM, there is no evidence that employees are gaining in terms of freedom and becoming independent of organizations unless they become entrepreneurs (see Chapter 5). Psychological contracts do not seem to change positively in any country, mainly because those who are employers have a large pool of talented but marginalized people available. This seems to happen almost everywhere. Certain social and professional circles fabricate talents through education, wealth, upbringing (family background) and any other forms. Most marginalized people come from North Africa, the Middle East, the Far East and Central America.

As of 2015, the daily number of North Africans (and other Africans who reach Libya, where they depart to Europe) who risk their lives to reach Europe is a disgrace. They are trafficked by both their own people and Europeans, to whom they pay a considerable amount of money and are sent in boats to Europe. They often reach the sea border between Italy and Africa, where they expect to be saved by European volunteers in the middle of the sea or else near Lampedusa, an Italian island nearby. Many die on their way for lack of food, water or not knowing how to swim (when the boat is deliberately sunk to erase signs of the traffickers). The EU has been somewhat slow in taking measures to stop the suffering of these victims. Some European countries want to find the traffickers and destroy their boats, while others promote the reconstruction of their countries in Africa.

Until now, there have been no solutions and those who have arrived in Europe have generally been stuck in refugee camps while living at the mercy of European countries. These refugees, when interviewed, have high hopes of being integrated and of transforming the world. While Europe has serious financial difficulties and unclear social policies, these refugees dream about unifying the world through the lenses of their own democratic concepts.

The same kind of human traffic occurs in many other places (including in some regions of the USA), but not in such large numbers or such an uncontrolled manner. It is worth commenting on those refugees from Central America traveling to the USA because of some of the political measures helping them to be integrated in the USA and the repatriation policies being implemented. The USA has had to invest millions to care for the health and paperwork of these victims. However, if those who have to return continue suffering in their own countries, this is a strong sign that better international development programs need to be implemented to engage them in the reconstruction of their countries through government agreements (since there are laws against intervening in other countries, and sometimes volunteers cannot do anything before the governments of both countries agree and approve any help).

Critical Perspective

This chapter reflected upon whether employees in various countries could become autonomous, and it seems that only a minority – namely property owners – can be less reliant upon organizations. However, for most people, including in the Nordic countries where discourses of transparency and equal opportunities reign, there remain forms of subordination, inequality and various relations of social power.

For every country, this chapter on TM and the identification of talents tried to offer a discussion of how employees interconnect with each other and how they are collectively responsible for each other by questioning whether psychological contracts have changed positively. There are no indications of positive changes in this regard, mainly because wealthier countries have a surplus of people (including immigrants and refugees) which gives employers a large pool of talented people who are ready to work and accept almost any type of informal psychological contract. We saw in the last chapter that even many professionalized British citizens have no 'contracts' (i.e., zero-hours contracts), which obliges them to take several jobs at the same time or else during the summer when they are not paid by the hour. If national citizens who are tied by law to their countries with the right to vote are not able to claim that they are being treated fairly and work under conditions of subordination and inequality, then clearly immigrants and refugees not tied by laws will not be in a position to change this situation.

Regarding trafficked people who are repatriated, governments need to find agreements, lower social tensions and increase international development programs. They need to increase the number of talented experts (see Reis, 2016) who are able to respect other cultures and various other relations of social power.

Utopia

It is possible that refugees would like to find Utopia and live under such a social order (which is a clear order) until their mental and physical health are re-established. However, it is known that refugees are sometimes rebels, that they have nonrealistic expectations of being accepted as they are, and that they are used to their own environments (in Africa and other places). Their understanding of Western cultures is limited, giving place to self-legitimization for rebellion and victimization. These reflect other urgent government measures that need to implement regarding the consensus for refugees and their understanding of their new lives in Western countries. These measures involve ways of integrating people by accepting their own differences and those of others in their host countries. Governments who have such lawful authority should not leave this to the will of opportunists, who may exploit refugees with promises of work, etc.

Refugees have their own unique knowledge and identities, and it is probably the case that they would like to share these with one another other in the camps in which they live and that they can be responsible for each other. They can be integrated in their host countries in many ways through diversity management development programs which have dignity for humanity. Al Ariss et al. (2014) suggest that there is a need for TM to place a greater emphasis on diversity management in order to attract minorities. However, in the present global economy it appears that there is a need to place emphasis on attracting the new talents of refugees in many parts of the world in a dignified way and without social tensions between themselves and their host countries.

References

Al Ariss, A., Cascio, W. F. & Jaap, P. (2014) Talent management: current theories and future research directions, *Journal of World Business*, 49, 173–179.

Farndale, E., Pai, A., Sparrow, P. & Scullion, H. (2013) Balancing individual and organizational goals in global talent management: a mutual-benefits perspective, *Journal World of Business*, 49, 204–214.

McDonnell, A., Collings, D. G. & Burgess, J. (2012) Guest editors' note: talent management in the Asia Pacific, *Asia Pacific Journal of Human Resources*, 50(4), 391–398.

Reis, C. (2016) The remote work of managers working cross-culturally, *Journal of Applied Management and Entrepreneurship* (in press).

Reis, C. & Baruch, Y. (Eds.) (2013) *Careers without Borders: Critical Perspectives*, New York: Routledge.

Ronen, S. & Shenkar, O. (1985) Clustering countries on attitudinal dimensions: a review and synthesis, *Academy of Management Review*, 10: 435–454.

4 In Search Of Talented Leaders

Introduction

The aim of this chapter is to understand the self-identity of leaders within the main topics of this book, careers and TM. For the purpose of the study in this chapter, leaders are assumed to be 'talents' and to have 'successful careers'. In order to analyze leaders' self-identities in their careers, and with respect to TM, empirical data were collected for this chapter.

I begin by explaining two self-identity theories with contrasting understandings of how leaders become 'talents': the theories of Carl Rogers and Jacques Lacan. Carl Rogers' theory of the self is known mainly in the field of individual psychotherapy and is neglected in management. However, Rogers' contribution to the self, as applied to TM, is of major importance because the theory views the best side of individuals. In other words, *assuming that leaders are not disturbed in their social environment, they should produce practical positive actions when leading others.*

Lacan's theory, developed after Rogers', focuses on the process of the desired self. *Lacan's theory applied to leaders is a negative irrationality in which actions are not always positive.* While Rogers' theory is *supportive*, seeing individuals producing their best, Lacan's theory is *restorative*, seeing individuals producing irrational actions to get what they miss in their lives.

The next sections introduce a discussion of Rogers' and Lacan's theories followed by a research review of contemporary self-identities theories. This follows a review of management and leadership, and an empirical study of leaders and how they see their self-identities.

Carl Rogers on the Self and the Concept of a Self-actualizing Tendency

Early on, Rogers' (1959) concept of the self was developed with individual bodies which were not necessarily human beings, such as microorganisms, and how they interacted. Rogers developed the concept of a *self-actualizing tendency*, which is a crucial driver for individual bodies to *survive independently.* This independence and self-sufficiency is *directional rather than instructional.*

Therefore, this concept assumes that a self-actualizing tendency is positively regarded as a constructive action and that it is present in all individual living bodies: 'It is a direction, not a destination' (Rogers, 1959: 186). Another important characteristic of the concept of the self-actualizing tendency is that it *can be suppressed* but not destroyed, unless the organism is destroyed (Rogers, 1977). The self-actualizing tendency is consistent with the need for positive self-regard from others, and this involves symbolized experiences of the self.

Later, Rogers introduces the concept of *gains on social standards of value*. However, this new concept opposes the initial theory of a self-actualizing tendency because it is not fluid or engaged in movement as is the case with the self-actualizing tendency. This means that *gains on social standards of value* disturb the individual's awareness of positive self-regard. *Consequently, the individual becomes twisted between his/her self-actualizing tendency of his/her own individual body, which is fluid, and the gains on social standards of value.*

Thus, for Rogers (1961), the ideal individual is open to both of these concepts which the body trusts. Individuals enter a selective process which is driven *without conscious awareness* and which usually results in positive actions. Rogers did not deny that this can result in maladaptive behavior, namely incongruent feelings of anxiety, confusion and tension. However, he did not focus on conflicts or destructive individuals (Rogers, 1959). In summary, Rogers (1977) sees individuals as: 'capable of evaluating the outer and inner situation, understanding herself in its context, making constructive choices as to the next steps in life, and acting on those choices' (15).

Rogers (1977)later revised the incongruence of both concepts and explained why the self-actualizing tendency functions. First, the self-actualizing tendency is conditional and works when individuals reach the standards that others have applied to them. Second, these standards are created by others and are created without keeping each individual in mind. Most individuals are able to achieve them, and they are therefore able to maintain a sense of worth.

With these concepts applied to TM and leadership, leaders tend to self-actualize their potential talent by evaluating their situations in their context and are capable of making and acting through constructive choices.

Lacan on the Self

Lacan's theory suggests the process of the desired self and this process may result in individuals' irrational behavior. Lacan's theory (1977, 1988 and 1991) was derived from Freudian concepts. Freud introduced the idea of the human self being divided between the conscious and unconscious. For Freud, actions, thoughts, beliefs and the concepts of 'self' are shaped by the unconscious and its motivations and desires.

Lacan reinterprets Freud in light of structuralist and post-structuralist theories and questions the ideal self; the goal was to strengthen the self through conscious and for rational identity to become more powerful than the unconscious. However, in Lacan's interpretation, the self can never adopt this position whenever the unconscious controls it. The reason for this is that, for Lacan, *the self is simply an illusion resulting from the unconscious.* This concept derives from Lacan's essay titled *The Mirror Stage* in which he was interested in how infants acquire the illusion of the self. Lacan notes that the unconscious is symbolic and verbal, and that it is either condensed in metaphor or displaced in metonymy. This saw the result that Lacan's theory claims that *the unconscious is the ruler of human existence and is structured in the same way as language.*

This concept is important in the process of developing self-identities. Lacan sees this process as an illusion created by a misperception of the relation between the body and the self. Lacan's language is always about loss or absence, whereby words are only needed when the desired object is absent. This development occurs when the infant does not master its body, resulting in fragmented experiences. It is in this situation when the mirror stage gains importance, and it happens when individuals compare themselves to other bodies. The infant looks at its reflection and then back to the imagined self – the mirror process or a reflected image. However, this concept brings forth the notion that self-identity is a mirrored identification and that it is a misrecognition of the individual which is not necessarily real to others.

In light of Lacan's theory, talented leaders may have an extreme egocentric imaginary perception of themselves which is not necessarily useful when they lead.

Various Concepts of Self-Identity

The previous sections presented a clear theoretical framework with two theories that are in opposition to each other. However, in recent years, concepts of self-identity have been conceptualized across disciplines, making it difficult to find a common discourse (Burke, 2003).

In organizations studies, the field of self-identity has become a challenging debate, since it requires researchers to recognize ambiguity, tensions and dynamics by offering a framework for variations without being fixated upon rigid ideas and approaches. Haslam and Reicher (2006) see identity studies as important in 'leading to significant theoretical and practical advances in the study of almost every aspect of organizational life' (135). For example, Stets (1995) view of self-identities emphasizes personal characteristics not necessarily shared by others, such as assertiveness, honor and trustworthiness. Other authors, such as Kuhn (2006), concentrate on 'self-reflexivity and [what is] discursively understood' (1340); Scott et al. (1998) viewed identity as an anchor but they also emphasize the shifting targets for the identification of individuals; Watson (2008) discusses how people try to sustain a positive and authentic sense of self in a context of contradictory demands; Collinson (2003) is strongly concerned with essentialism and avers that there is a 'dualistic tendency to artificially separate individuals from society, mind from body, rationality from emotion' (527); Stets and Burke (2000) suggest that 'a complete theory of the self would consider both the role and the group bases of identity as well as identities based in the person that provide stability across groups, roles and situations' (234).

All these authors' views on self-identities suggest: insecurity and anxiety in individuals' experiences where subjectivity is privileged and identity is reshaped; the role of language and discourse in constituting an individual subject that does not exist outside language; the strong sense of continuity and security in maintaining a credible self-narrative; the modification of possible selves to achieve goals; normalization and a sense of belonging to groups or other institutions. These views of self-identity will be considered in the main analytical framework of the theories of Roger versus those of Lacan in the following sections.

Leadership and Management

The literature in the field of leadership is extensive (for reviews, see Andersen, 2000; Bryman, 1996; Dubrin, 2001; House and Aditay, 1997; Palmer and Hardy, 2000; Yukl, 1989). There has also been extensive research comparing leaders and leadership, and managers and management (Barker, 1997; Fagiano, 1997; Kotter, 1990; Mintzberg, 1998; Zaleznik, 1977).

Leadership implies that an individual has the vision, creativity and inspiration for the business in question as well as the capacity for cooperation and networking, and for organizing effective teamwork. Leadership is seen as inspirational (Mintzberg, 1988) and visionary (Kotter, 1990; Fagiano, 1997), while management in opposition to leadership is controlling, coordinating and directing, formal, scientific, structured, systematic and bureaucratic (e.g., Mintzberg, 1998; Kotter, 1990; Fagiano, 1997). There are also research discussions about the characteristics of being a leader versus being a manager (e.g., Dubrin, 2001). The leader is usually a visionary, the one with creativity (Bartlett and Ghoshal, 1995), as opposed to the reactive, analytical and structured manager who responds to the requests of others (Larson et al., 1986).

This chapter is based on the question of how managers perceive their self-identities, talent and careers. Therefore, I postpone taking a firm theoretical stance on, first, whether self-identities must be important in leadership and, if so, why, and second, the meaning given by those talking about it. It is acknowledged that the topics of leadership, TM and careers are not entirely new, but leaders' views of their self-identities in this respect remain unexplored. Leaders' self-identities help us understanding TM and careers.

The Study

This study involves understanding the orientations of leaders' self-identities in various organizational settings with more than 1,000 employees. In total, the researcher interviewed 25 leaders from whom the following categories were integrated: 5 in the 'needy' category, 7 in the 'restorative' category and 13 in the 'mixed' category. In this study, all the managers had organizational decision-making autonomy on social responsibility issues. The benefit of using these diverse settings in this study lies in the ability to allow the researcher to compare the extent to which participants' responses were similar on the basis of their shared occupation as leaders, as well as where particular issues of context appeared to make a difference.

The interviews were in-depth and open-ended (Kvale, 1996). While pre-ordained boundaries were not fixed, the interview highlighted key issues of the present study. It is worth noting that most of the interviewees were able to develop, by themselves, the broad themes proposed at the beginning of the interview. In these cases, the role of the interviewer was merely to ensure that the interviewee was talking about issues related to the subjects under investigation.

All the managerial interviews were conducted by first asking the managers about their jobs and careers and how they might describe their own self-identities. When the research was conducted, the participants were questioned as to what extent their self-identities were specific to managers' leadership abilities and in being recognized as a talent by their peers.

Data and Interpretation

The analysis and interpretation of the data begins with the first interview, since human beings are unable to merely collect data but always try to make sense of information. However, the researcher's first step towards a more systematic understanding of the fieldwork notes in the context of the research questions begins with the process of writing up a transcript. In general, researchers begin by first telling the story to themselves; only then do they initiate the process of writing it up for their scientific community. During this process, one must consider how to make sense of the managers' interviews and how to select extracts from them.

This stage of data analysis follows the proposal of Miles and Huberman (1994): when one works with texts or less well-organized displays, one can often note recurring patterns, themes or 'gestalts', which pull together many separate pieces of data (Miles and Huberman, 1994: 246). One has to recognize that no absolute and definitive version of a story can be given: 'There are only always different versions of different, not the same, stories, even when the same site is studied' (Denzin and Lincoln 1994: 506).

The issue of how the themes and aspects developed during this step is organized in conjunction with what is told by other managers in an interesting way. Since the researcher has implicitly to decide what will be written, namely 'how one moves from a blank page (or screen) to a written text, one sentence after another, building an emergent, reflexive interpretation of the subject matter at hand' (Denzin and Lincoln, 1994: 504), the task of the writer is now to create interest and expectation in the reader.

The managers' accounts provide information as to how they see their world while working for organizations. Denzin argues: 'In the social sciences there is only interpretation. Nothing speaks for itself' (500). The analysis of managers' accounts mainly uses the theories on the self of Rogers (1959 and 1977) as contrasted with Lacan's theory (1977, 1988 and 1991). In this study, the researcher evaluated a text in terms of its ability to reveal multiple meanings that produce categories in opposition with each other. The next account is presented with an analysis that demonstrates how the researcher elaborated the following categories:

> I cannot control many situations in this business. I have tremendous worries but I cannot let my employees notice these feelings. I need to develop an image of serenity.

According to the perspective of this manager, leading is about presenting a self-identity image of security. The analysis unveils that this manager worries about leading people and about the efficacy of this projected self-image. By contrast, other managers spoke about convincing employees of credible stories of socially responsible actions and not worrying about what would happen.

In Table 4.1 meanings of own self-identities when leading have been noted as types of observations while leading individuals. The observations and key factors identified as constraining or enabling managers' understanding of their self-identities that inductively generated categories (King, 1994).

Findings

Patterns in the data revealed the existence of three different categories of how managers made sense of and talked about their self-identities and leadership in their current organizational settings as well as in the broader world of management and social context. Thus, meanings are captured in a patterned manner which permits an examination of differences and convergences.

These categories do not mean that there are three groups of managers, but rather that managers across sectors, genders, ages and types of business talked about leadership in management in these three broadly different ways. While clearly aware of alternatives, most people more strongly identified with one approach rather than with the others. Recognizing the paradoxes and

Table 4.1

Key factor	Observations in managers' accounts while leading others
Meanings of own self-identities when leading	Worried individuals vs. confident individuals
	Pacific vs. disturbed individuals
	Recognition of being a talent vs. no recognition

processes of identifying that people bring to their own self-identities, the interviewees could be broadly categorized into one of the three categories that captured their understanding of their leadership talent. Common characteristics of categories and slipping backwards and forwards between categories are recognized, but these three kinds do capture the involvedness of managers' self-identities as leaders.

Next, the three categories are outlined and then followed by a discussion of the significance of self-identities as leaders: 'needy', 'restorative' and 'mixed'.

The Needy

This category was identified by the themes interviewees expanded upon about their own self-identity as the type of person who worries; this means that these managers spoke about leading others, and their actions, by presenting a self-image which did not correspond with what they were feeling. These five managers described these feelings in situations they did not control. For example:

> In situations I do not control I cannot trust anyone. I feel bad and I cannot let anyone enter my office.
>
> When I feel there is the possibility of being spotted, as soon as I arrive at my hotel, I ask the hotel manager to change my room number in their listings.

According to Rogers' theory, leaders in this category are constantly trying to deal with worries and anxieties in order to reach the fullest functioning self/ social conditions of self-worth. Rogers' concept of the actualizing tendency becomes important within this variation, since it is a crucial drive for the survival and achievement of leaders' independence. However, when social conditions become a limitation, as is the case in the above examples, as well as when individuals do not attain the social condition of self-worth, they may engage in maladjusted behavior. In these examples, the manager did not adjust to the physical conditions and made a special request by changing access to his/her space in his/her office or hotel room.

These insecurities derive from the manager's relationship with the environment and his/her need to control the surrounding conditions. When individuals do not control certain situations, and in order to achieve their fullest functioning self, they may engage in extremely peculiar requests, and even in threatening behavior.

According to the Lacannian approach, these leaders see their external world as represented in a mirror through which the self is displayed. In the above examples, their concerns were to create a desired reflection for others.

> This reflection must of course support that person's desire to see the most flattering reflection, but in such a way that it appears as reality. This is brought about by every person's inherent insecurity and seeking for the ideal self.
>
> (Crowther, 2006: 65)

In light of Lacan's theory, leaders perceive themselves as being in danger or else destroyed by their illusion of their most desired self-image embodied in anxiety and insecurity.

The Restorative

The themes that the interviewees developed about their own self-identities in this category were about justifying a credible story for critical events. These seven managers described how they played hide and seek with their own identities while leading others. For example:

> Sometimes I have to tell bad news but I do not want to disappoint the people I lead. In my view telling bad news does not inspire them to achieve results. I tell a story and some facts are hidden for the sake of the profitability of our projects.

Following a Rogerian approach, individuals adjust to their fullest functioning self through discourse, and they may juggle with 'languages' and meanings, causing confusing behaviors that are full of subjectivism. The Rogerian approach sees individuals as having the opportunity to adjust to the fullest functioning self by narrating the story that they believe and returning through this self-development to their condition of worth and the concept of an actualizing tendency whereby social conditions are open to (re)interpretation. If issues of credibility are raised, it may place the individual in a state of maladjustment since they may try to secure different versions of their stories.

Following Lacan's theory, this production of subjectivities seemed to have satisfied individuals who identify with what is lacking in their environment. In Lacan's theory, the recognition of what is lacking is a crucial development for the mirror stage (Easthope and McGowan, 2004) and represents a pleasurable victory for these leaders. They believe that they can lead others by not mentioning/hiding facts about the projects named to this category.

In the Lacannian approach, '[t]he wish to appear as a highly competent and capable person and the more difficult the activity in which (s)he is perceived to be engaged the closer that image relates to the ideal self' (Crowther, 2006: 70). If achievement is reached, it reinforces the desired self-identity (mirror image). In the example above, they wish to appear as highly capable human beings by engaging in leadership.

The Mixed

Interviewees in this category were identified by the themes related to 'disclosing suspicious practices'. These managers (13) described these concerns connected with what they saw as losing their jobs. For example:

> It does not cross my mind to disclose any malpractice that I am aware [of]. I don't want to disappoint those I lead.

According to the Rogerian approach, leaders in this category deviate from the fullest functioning self/social conditions of worth in order to meet what is expected of them. This is the case when leaders begin disclosing suspicious practices which are supposed to be common to all involved.

Lacan's theory sees such leaders as achieving the desired self-identity and engaging in the individuation process through such schemes. According to Crowther (2002), '[i]f this image is accepted by the readers of the script then, because the author determines and perceives his/her identity from viewing it upon the mirror of the world, the author can also accept this image' (65). The Lacannian approach fits leaders at the unconscious level, without the existence of a relationship between the signifier and signified, and with an emphasis on the relations of value. In this sense, enthusiasm and lucidity may not have much worth for individuals who fit a mirrored self-identity.

Conclusion

Self-identities are drivers for leaders and, consequently, leadership. According to Ghosh (2008), workplace decisions are affected by both an organization's corporate values and person-based convictions, but some individuals have a strong sense of the self; 'it matters little where they work' (Bolman and Deal, 2008: 399). Moreover, in times of crisis 'the most important responsibility is not to answer every question or get every decision right' (Bolman and Deal, 2008: 409). *Therefore, following these ideas, managers see their own leadership in the same way as they manage their self-identities.*

It was not the aim of this study to provide an explanatory model. The sample of managers used in this study is only indicative of managers' leadership and self-identities in different settings. Although the leaders in this study work in different institutional settings, it is possible that their self-identities and notions of leadership are shaped by other determinants, because the degree of shared notions may vary among cultural contexts (Hofstede and Hofstede, 2005).

Global leadership development is used in organizations to identify talent and who to develop, and aims to have the right kind of leadership. Conceptual models have been elaborated (e.g., Sloan, Hazucha and Kaywyk, 2003) in this respect, which include clarifying the globalization strategy, defining global leadership roles and requirements, and designing TM systems. Future research could explore how leaders believe they become talents and that they are taking the right decisions without critically questioning their own self-identities, beliefs, thinking and understanding (Argyris, 1991; Burgoyne, 2002).

Are the careers of these leaders useful? If, according to Rogers' theory, they produce practical positive actions when leading others, they are useful. However, if leaders focus on the process of the desired self as viewed by Lacan, this turns into a negative irrationality in which actions are not always positive.

From a critical perspective, none of the categories identified in this study, namely 'needy', 'restorative' and 'mixed', presents leaders who are free from subordinating others to inequality and relations of social power for the most bizarre reasons. Therefore, taking into account that their aim should be, in theory, to be collectively responsible for organizations and others, leaders' practices are always questionable and should be frequently audited – such is human nature.

In *Utopia*, leaders' differentiation in terms of ways of leading others was not conceptualized and it was assumed that they were taking responsibility for others and the perfect social order. Nowadays, and only when there is suspicious business behavior or concrete corruption, are leaders subject to auditing. Otherwise, as in the Utopia, it is assumed that our leaders are taking good care of our organizations and societies.

References

Andersen, J. A. (2000) Leadership and leadership research. In D. F. Dahiya (Ed.), *Current Issues in Business Disciplines, Volume 5: Management II.* 2267–2287

Argyris, C. (1991) Teaching smart people how to learn, *Harvard Business Review*, 69, 99–109.

Barker, R. A. (1997) How can we train leaders if we do not know what leadership is? *Human Relations*, 50(4), 343–362.

Barker, R. (2001) The nature of leadership, *Human Relations*, 54, 469–493.

Bartlett, C. & Ghoshal, S. (1995) Changing the role of top management beyond systems to people, *Harvard Business Review*, May–June, 132–133.

Bolman, L. G. & Deal, T. E. (2008) *Reframing Organizations: Artistry, Choice, and Leadership*, New York: John Wiley & Sons.

Bryman, A. (1996) Leadership in organizations. In S. Clegg, C. Hardy & W. Nord (Eds.), *Handbook of Organization Studies*. London: Sage.

Burgoyne, J. G. (2002) Learning theory and the construction of the self: what kinds of people do we create through the theories of learning that we apply to their development? In M. A. Pearn (Ed.), *Individual Differences and Development in Organizations*, New York: John Wiley & Sons.

Burke, P. J. (2003) Relationships among Multiple Identities. In P. J. Burke, T. J. Owens, R. T. Serpe & P. A. Thoits (Eds.), *Advances in Identity Theory and Research*, New York: Kluwer Academic/Plenum.

Collinson, D. L. (2003) Identities and insecurities: selves at work, *Organization*, 10(3), 527–547.

Crowther, D. (2002) *A Social Critique of Corporate Reporting*. Aldershot: Ashgate.

Crowther, D. (2006) Psychoanalysis and auditing. In S. Clegg, C. Hardy & W. Nord (Eds.), *Handbook of Organization Studies*. London: Sage.

Denzin, N. & Lincoln, Y. (1994) The fifth moment. In *Handbook of Qualitative Research*. Thousand Oaks, CA: Sage.

Dubrin, A. (2001) *Leadership: Research Findings, Practice and Skills*. Boston, Mass: Houghton Mifflin.

Easthope, A. & McGowan, K. (2004) *A Critical and Cultural Theory Reader*. Toronto and Buffalo, NY: University of Toronto Press.

Fagiano, D. (1997) Managers vs. leaders: a corporate fable, *Management Review*, 10, 5–6.

Ghosh, D. (2008) Corporate values, workplace decisions and ethical standards of employees, *Journal of Managerial Issues*, 20(1), 68–90.

Haslam, S. A. & Reicher, S. (2006) Rethinking the psychology of tyranny: the BBC Prison Study, *British Journal of Social Psychology*, 45, 1–40.

Hofstede, G. & Hofstede, G. J. (2005) *Cultures and Organizations: Software of the Mind*, New York: McGraw-Hill.

House, R. & Aditay, R. (1997) The social scientific study of leadership: quo vadis? *Journal of Managament*, 23(3), 409–473.

King, N. (1994) The qualitative research interview. In C. Cassel & G. Symon (Eds), *Qualitative Methods in Organisational Research: A Practical Guide*. London: Sage. 14–36.

Kotter, J. (1990) *Force for Change: How Leadership Differs From Management*. New York: Free Press.

Kuhn, T. (2006) A demented work ethic and a 'lifestyle firm': discourses, identity, and workplace time commitments, *Organization Studies*, 27(9), 1339–1358.

Kvale, S. (1996) *Interviews*. London: Sage.

Lacan, J. (1977) The function and field of speech and language in psychoanalysis. In *Écrits*. New York: Norton. 30–113.

Lacan, J. (1988) *The Seminars of Jacques Lacan Book II: The Ego in Freud's Theory and in the Technique of Psychoanalysis 1954–1955* (trans. S. Tomaselli). New York: Cambridge University Press.

Lacan, J. (1991) *The Seminars of Jacques Lacan Book I: Freud's Papers on Technique 1953–1954* (trans. J. Forrester). New York: W. W. Norton & Co.

Larson, L., Bussom, R., Vicars, W. & Jauch, L. (1986) Proactive versus reactive manager: is the dichotomy realistic? *Journal of Management Studies*, 23(4), 385–400.

McAdams, D. P. (1996) Personality, modernity, and the social self: a contemporary framework for studying persons, *Psychology Inquiry*, 7, 295–321.

Miles, M. B. and Huberman, A. M. (1994) *Qualitative Data Analysis: An Expanded Sourcebook*. Beverly Hills, CA: Sage.

Mintzberg, H. (1988) Opening up the definition of strategy. In J. Quinn, H. Mintzberg & R. M. James, *The Strategy Process*. Englewood Cliffs, NJ: Prentice Hall.

Mintzberg, H. (1998) Covert leadership: notes on managing professionals, *Harvard Business Review*, November–December, 140–147.

Palmer, I. & Hardy, C. (2000) *Thinking about Management*. London: Sage

Thomas, R., Linstead, A. & Thomas, R. (2002) Losing the plot? Middle managers and identity, *Organization*, 9(1), 71–93.

Rogers, C. (1959) A theory of therapy, personality and interpersonal relationships as developed in the client-centered framework. In S. Koch (Ed.), *Psychology: A Study of a Science. Vol. 3: Formulations of the Person and the Social Context*. New York: McGraw-Hill.

Rogers, C. (1961) *On Becoming a Person: A Therapist's View of Psychotherapy*. London: Constable.

Rogers, C. (1977) *On Personal Power: Inner Strength and Its Revolutionary Impact*. New York: Delacorte Press.

Scott, C. R., Corman, S. R., et al. (1998) Development of a structurational model of identification in the organization, *Communication Theory*, 8(3): 298–336.

Stets, J. E. (1995) Role identities and person identities: gender identity, mastery identity, and controlling one's partner, *Sociological Perspectives*, 38(2), 129–150.

Stets, J. E. & Burke, P. J. (2000) Identity theory and social identity theory, *Social Psychology Quarterly*, 63(3), 224–237.

Watson, T. J. (2008) Managing identity: identity work, personal predicaments and structural circumstances, *Organization*, 15(1), 121–143.

Yukl, G. (1989) Managerial leadership: a review of theory and research, *Journal of Management*, 15, 251–289.

Zaleznik, A. (1977) Managers and leaders: are they different?, *Harvard Business Review*, May–June, 67–68.

5 Global Entrepreneurs Dealing with Business Remotely

Introduction

This chapter examines how entrepreneurs manage their business through remote methods of management (i.e., by not being physically present in the place where their business is active). Remote methods of management are interesting for the field of careers because, as I have already argued in Chapter 2, education and government policies give incentives for almost everyone to become an entrepreneur as a way to prevent unemployment. We are in a global economy, and at the same time, every entrepreneur has to become a global business person. Zahra (1999) saw the emergence of global entrepreneurs as the gateway to growth and prosperity, both in rich and in poor countries. Oviatt et al. (1995) saw global entrepreneurs as a growing phenomenon, with new domestic ventures becoming international.

There are different definitions of 'an entrepreneur', and in this chapter an entrepreneur is considered as an independent contractor rather than an employee of an organization with entrepreneurial work and skills. Therefore, in the area of TM, entrepreneurial skills can be discussed for those individuals with entrepreneurial skills but who work for an organization. Before discussing the actual work that entrepreneurs do – particularly when they manage projects remotely in a global economy – it is only proper to review the existing literature on remote management.

There are several debates on remote management, and these focus on virtual-team performance, conflicts, communication and cultural perspectives (e.g., Mulki et al., 2009; Maznevski and Chudoba, 2000), as well as on remote work and work–life balance (e.g., Baugh et al., 2013). However, little has been written on the remote managers' actual work.

The swift-trust theory has been applied to explaining global virtual teams. This theory defines a virtual team as 'a self-managed knowledge-work team, with distributed expertise, that forms and disbands to address a specific organizational goal' (Kristof et al., 1995). Although this characterization does not fit remote managers, as they manage individuals, it is useful to explore the swift-trust theory of virtual teams because there are limitations that can be applied to some remote work managers. According to Crisp and Jarvenpaa

(2013), trust is based on an early assumption that others on a given team are trustworthy, and this assumption is validated for each team member through the contribution of those team members to the performance of joint tasks, such as scheduling and monitoring. This is part of the actual work that remote managers do, and it has similar limitations to those resulting from the time and space differences that virtual teams confront in relying largely on electronic communications (e.g., Jarvenpaa, Shaw and Staples, 2004).

As indicated above, most of the previously published literature on these topics focuses on the challenges and barriers affecting virtual teams' effectiveness. *These studies explore a wide range of pertinent topics, but they all emphasize teams rather than individual entrepreneurs.* Such topics include virtual-team leadership (e.g., Zigurs, 2003), virtual-team task complexity (e.g., Bradford and Kozlowski, 2002), virtual-team technology and conflict resolution (e.g., Montoya-Weiss et al., 2001), and virtual teams and global entrepreneurship (e.g., Matlay and Westhead, 2005).

Remote management *is* explored in the communications literature, which looks at issues related to communications media by focusing mostly on virtual teams. For example, such literature claims that, to be successful, remote managers must create highly synchronous environments with no delays (Kirkman and Mathieu, 2005). Following this line of thought, one might suppose, for example, that video conference communication tools could provide highly synchronized meetings, but one might also argue that these conversations take longer and require more explanation because of missing cues. Moreover, the communications literature at present suggests that e-mails, conference calls and text messages do not provide the same experience as a physical, social presence. The authors of some of these studies assert that, just because '[t]he volume of communication is frequently greater in remote work arrangements, this doesn't necessarily mean that the communication is more effective; electronic communication suffers from a lack of contextual cues and norms' (Mulki et al., 2009: 65). Meanwhile, other authors contend that the lack of attentiveness, the absence of contextual cues and norms, and the potential for misinterpretation can foment conflict (Jong et al., 2008).

Focusing on communications issues, Kirkman and Mathieu (2005: 704) propose the concept of *informational value*, stating that 'when members employ technologies that convey rich, valuable information, then their exchanges are less virtual than when they employ technologies that provide less valuable information'. The idea of determining which information is valuable was proposed by Jong et al. (2008), who added that virtual management does not offer a reliable way of managing a business; instead, the communicated data can differ for each member, can be manipulated by persons at any time, and is very variable and therefore unreliable. Based on these conclusions, one might surmise that managing remotely involves a higher level of complexity than hands-on project/site management. The present study furthers this discussion by examining important insights from the literature on managerial work and connects these with the entrepreneurial work.

These writings are usually centered on administrative tasks or instrumental aspects, such as budgets, structures, performance, compensation and rewards (e.g., Dubrin, 2001; Fagiano, 1997; Mintzberg, 1998; Zaleznik, 1977). However, practices involving social dimensions, such as informal talks in a cafeteria, are often excluded from mainstream management discussions (e.g., Alvesson and Sveningsson, 2003); after all, remote managers cannot deploy such informal practices as managerial tactics. Meanwhile, Alvesson and Sveningsson's (2003) study found that the social side of managers' work is crucial to positive outcomes from their interactions with local people with whom they deal or, in other words, with those who implement the hands-on aspects of managers' projects.

The literature says very little about remote entrepreneurs' daily work dynamics. This chapter focuses on the work of those who are entrepreneurs and deal with business remotely. Before discussing the actual work that entrepreneurs do – particularly when they manage projects remotely in a global economy – it is only proper to review the existing literature on remote management (see Reis, 2016).

Careers of Global Entrepreneurs Working Remotely

Global entrepreneurs represent a phenomenon which started in the 1990s with the emergence of the internet and global economics. During this decade, it seemed that it was almost a matter of destiny for global entrepreneurs to be dealing with businesses remotely.

Hisrich (2012) says that global entrepreneurs found a way of entering foreign markets without a large equity investment through owning foreign subsidiaries. This is a frequent mode of foreign direct investment and needs supervision, which is mostly done remotely. Kuratko (2013) sees global entrepreneurs as open-minded, able to see an opportunity and as having different perspectives within a unified focus. They are capable of rising above national differences to envision how to compete globally. Gibbons et al. (2014) perceive global entrepreneurs as having common traits. They are clear about their business vision, exhibit openness to cultural diversity and tolerance for ambiguous environments, as well as having aspirations to achieve. Ayisi (2013) claims that there are two types of people who become entrepreneurs: those who are capable of identifying new commercial opportunities and those who see and exploit practical, existing opportunities.

Applying the theory of careers capital's three dimensions, defined as knowing-why, knowing-how and knowing-whom (DeFillippi and Arthur, 1994; Inkson and Arthur, 2001; Eby et al., 2003), another perspective can be developed about global entrepreneurs.

The global entrepreneurs' knowing-why career capital dimension relies on their self-identification with this type of work. These entrepreneurs are detached from institutionalized norms and other forms of behavior; they are somehow free from internal institutional pressures. Entrepreneurs are usually their own bosses, self-confident in that they believe in their ability to lead their business (Jones and Lichtenstein, 2000; Inkson and Arthur, 2001). Entrepreneurs search for every opportunity to make their wishes happen, which is in line with the concept of internal career issues of the protean career (Hall, 1976). However, they live in societies and they are not completely unrestricted from the external and political demands of structures and laws (see Reis and Baruch, 2013).

There are many available biographies of male entrepreneurs who are presented as superstars. However, few female entrepreneurs have been portrayed as independent superstars (see Reis, 2010). This chapter presents a typical interview, which deserves consideration because of the risky choices women take (as do men, but women have less social encouragement) even when they live in rich countries and have access to different types of government programs and other financial incentives.

Another career capital dimension is knowing-how, which focuses mainly on individual skills and knowledge required to perform at the level of organizational standards (Defillippi and Arthur, 1994). Entrepreneurs, before entering any business that they lead, either have the required knowledge, experience or skills (which they sometimes name 'luck').

The third career capital dimension, knowing-whom, is more complex and is very important in the context of remote work. It discusses all professionally and personally relevant networks and contacts in their business careers (DeFillippi and Arthur, 1994; Parker and Arthur, 2000; Borgatti and Cross, 2003). It is related social capital (Burt, 1992; Raider and Burt, 1996), meaning a network of relationships useful to entrepreneurs regarded as assets for their business (Jones and DeFillippi, 1996; Nahapiet and Ghoshal, 1998; Adler and Kwon, 2002).

Women Global Entrepreneurs

There are several ways in which women can engage in global entrepreneurship, and one of them is by dealing with business remotely. For example, Sheryl Sandberg (2013) suggested ways of doing virtual work for women who stay at home. Women, in difficult contexts with few resources, can engage in global entrepreneurship, but only if they are knowledgeable of other business cultures, and have certain conditions of freedom and time on their own.

Much has been written regarding virtual work and non-work demands in terms of flexible work and remote work which permit women to manage their own time in a way that is more personally effective but not necessarily less demanding. There are global initiatives to this end (see World Bank, 2013) that are trying to bring women together within their businesses' social networks, but they may have to work individually and strategically very hard to get the right business networks. Although, nowadays, it is possible to contact anyone by virtual modes of communication, prestigious and influential contacts may require personal introductions and social status. This virtually connected trend will require that women – in the same way as men as regards global entrepreneurship – leave their homes and move geographically for meetings to build further business knowledge and networks.

Women who Chose to become Global Entrepreneurs

Many people end up in entrepreneurship because of their family upbringing as entrepreneurs or as a way out of an oppressive situation regarding their careers in the corporate world. Others became entrepreneurs because of their social life circumstances, because they did not enjoy studying, or because they could not find a good job as an employee. In this section, I will present the biography of a woman who had a choice between the corporate world and being an entrepreneur. Her life story is encouraging in the sense that she sees herself as a free person with social and political power as compared to those women who pursued careers in the corporate world.

Mary, a Superstar Global Entrepreneur

Mary is woman in her sixties who owns a small business enterprise, the Northeast's largest domestic and imported distributor of frozen food. She has 35 employees and her name, and the business sector, has been disguised for confidentiality purposes. She claims that her career as a global entrepreneur happened by accident. However, she worked hard, had the vision, took the risk and managed to invest her own capital in the company she worked for.

> When I was a student at University Y in 1974, and I answered a newspaper ad, they were looking for help. So I needed a job and I ended up here in New York and this is how I got to start at the very bottom of the company. I did the dirtiest and nastiest jobs and, over the course of the years, I learned different parts of business and I had an opportunity, after a couple of years to buy 10 percent of the business.

Mary explains how she became the sole owner of the business, though she included the previous owner in the business.

> So I did that and became a partner owner over the years. I learned more and more of the business, not just packing orders and even delivering orders to [Europe], but how to price, how to take care of the books and buy the products, etc. In 1980, the primary owner felt that the business should close and he and I made a deal that I would assume the debt of the business, which was 140,000 dollars, which was a lot of money. This was back in 1980, and I assumed the debt and bought the business for a dollar.

Initially, she made the first owner of the business her own main business partner and husband. The partnership ended after several years and she became the sole owner.

That's what I did, and I made my partner at the time, my life partner, my business partner as well, and so he and I grew the business over many years. Although I was always the president, then he and I got divorced seven years ago. I got him out of the business and I run it myself with the help of good people around me here.

However, she recognizes the importance of her partner and husband in the business mentorship process for her business.

My drive, more than anything, and I wouldn't say no because the prime owner of the business was a mentor to me in some ways. I learned a lot of things on my own and the hard way, but he was there for some guidance and again he gave me the opportunity so I look upon him as my mentor over the many years.

Mary explains her dedication to her business and, as with many entrepreneurs, she also thinks about the luck factor and how it was important, together with the opportunity.

I always worked for this business and never thought to change to another company. This is my first born child, I have two kids but the business was my first child so to speak. I have been much attached to it, and I have been very fortunate and I feel perseverance has been key to the success – but I feel definitely there is some luck out there as well as the opportunity.

Mary says she had no global strategy for her business. Her business philosophy was hard work, dedication and satisfaction in the creative process.

I cannot attribute it to any kind of strategy, and I would just say I was driven to excellence and that is where I got a lot of satisfaction in the creative process of growing a business and trying to make the best [food] distributor out there, and so in fact [my business] has been viewed as an industry leader for many years. We believe in life-long learning and continuous improvement, and are very committed and dedicated to this philosophy.

It is striking that, when she was 22 years old, she had the opportunity to work as a psychologist as an employee in a big company and yet she chose to continue her own business.

This was not my first job. When I was younger, I worked in a bakery and at the dentist's office, Dunking Donuts, and restaurants. I was only 22 years old when I started working here, so I was still young and I got my degree in psychology from University Y. I have always been very inter-ested in psychology, but by the time I got my degree I was so caught up in and enjoying my work here that I said 'Stick with this business'. In fact, I saw my own development within my business. I really don't know whether the corporate environment fosters that kind of person in development. It could have worked for the corporate world, but you know it is really exciting to be able to run your own life. You know there are many challenges and downs, but at the end of the day I am still doing what I want to do. I don't think a lot of people from the corporate world can say that – I don't think so.

Mary did volunteer work which was encouraged by her upbringing, and, in particular, by her mother. She is influential in local politics in relation to her industry. She says that this was a way of getting her ideas out for her own business and for personal excitement.

I was encouraged by my mom to run for various offices, and I have been on the board of education of several institutions. This volunteer work enabled me to see how other people did things. I got new ideas about doing things differently, and new approaches from many of the professionals that I met when I was in political office. I was engaged in many public and private partnerships regarding the economic development of corporations. I have been involved as a legislator for aspects of [the food distribution industry]. I have been doing this for many years, and this was a source of personal excitement and of getting new business ideas. This was a way of getting inspired.

Mary describes how her business company developed over the years, and in particularly when she started hiring employees. She had to manage the US and global economic crises, which touched all businesses and people in the USA. The way in which people work together changed with the crises and with the global economy.

When the company was very small, it was more about being friendly with everybody, and I still have family members working here today and it sometimes can be challenging to draw the line between the employer and the employee and the people that have been here for a long time. It can be interesting, at least to separate boundaries. It has changed. In the beginning, everybody was friendly and it was just small team work, group-working together and friends and then the business took off and grew a lot. At one point, we hired a professional company to come in and give us some guidelines, developing job descriptions and getting in writing what our HR policies are and computerizing them. At that point, we all developed more professional roles, but afterwards, when the economy started sinking, it affected our business and we had to cut down on some staff. People actually started working more closely with each other, me included, and not keeping a distance.

At the end of the interview, she realized how the global economy and the internet had brought about new ways of leading businesses. Nowadays, most entrepreneurs work remotely, leading businesses in other locations where they believe they need to be represented and have a registered venture in those other locations.

Critical Perspective

There is much to be investigated about the new careers of global entrepreneurs, and future research could use the biographies of global entrepreneurs who operate in several countries and contexts as well as different industries in order to study how they are innovating with their new ways of business leadership. Moreover, not much is known about global entrepreneurs dealing with business remotely.

From a critical perspective, global entrepreneurs are autonomous individuals who have the capacity to release certain forms of subordination, inequality and relations of social power. However, there is no evidence that they are doing the same for others who are their employees. Gibbons et al. (2014) claim that global entrepreneurs have integrity and are socially responsible, but scandals about failures in business and corruption continue to fill the pages in newspapers. Almost everyone who has an enterprise has it written somewhere for their clients that they are a socially responsible enterprise. However, most of these statements are merely fashionable discourses that they feel they must have in their adverts or other forms of agreements.

One type of 'green washing' is when money and time is invested in advertising rather than in practices that would really help the environment (Greenpeace USA, 2013). For example, some hotels advertise that they have the most advanced technology regarding environmental protection yet they treat their employees poorly. The issue is that social responsibility has an accounting research agenda and does not see this type of green washing, which uses people in the same way that products and services are used. They do not discuss issues in the field of human resources, probably because most auditors are accountants and do not know much about other research fields. While green washing is not new, its use has increased to meet consumers' demands with discourses that products or services are friendly to the environment when they are precisely the opposite (Karliner, 2007; Burdick, 2009). Most corporations, nowadays, are enforced by the law and regulatory agencies: in the USA, there is the Federal Trade Commission, in Canada, the Committee of Advertising Practice, and in the UK, the Broadcast Committee of Advertising Practices. Although there has been criticism of ineffective regulation, and an absence of external monitoring and verification, many corporations continue to use green washing to repair and legitimize their public image.

Utopia

In Utopia, family business entrepreneurs can exist just as they successfully exist in our own societies, but *private ownership did not exist*. However, the existence of women such as Mary, as was described in the above interview, would not be a possibility or could not co-exist because: 1) Utopia has a gender order, and 2) global entrepreneurs could not co-exist with Utopia's social system. They would disrupt the rules of Utopia by changing through innovation and creativity.

Therefore, the final question is whether the careers of global entrepreneurs are useful to our societies, in particular Western societies. They are very useful, but not everybody meets the conditions, personality, family background and upbringing and, in many cases, simply the opportunity (or 'luck', as they call it), that Mary meets. These global entrepreneurial careers – which governmental educational policies are trying to promote in many Western countries – are not for everybody.

There is also a lousy discourse on entrepreneurship in the area of TM. These are individuals with entrepreneurial skills who work for organizations as employees. Often, because they are energetic and have excellent or (mysterious) networks, they are awarded as superstars and talents. Some also claim that academics can engage in entrepreneurial work as contractors, that they can manage a portfolio of clients/universities as they became well-known superstars in their scientific areas. However, these situations may serve retired academics but not academics in general, since they are not even paid for their scientific publications.

References

Adler, P. S. & Kwon, S. W. (2002) Social capital: prospects for a new concept, *Academy of Management Review*, 27(1), 17–40.

Alvesson, M. & Sveningsson, S. (2003) Managers doing leadership: the extraordinarization of the mundane, *Human Relations*, 56(12), 1435–1439.

Ayisi, M. (2013) *The Global Entrepreneur*. Bloomington, IN: Authorhouse.

Baugh, G. S., Sullivan, S. E. & Carraher, S. M. (2013) Global Careers in the United States. In C. Reis & Y. Baruch (Eds.) *Careers Without Borders: Critical Perspectives*. New York: Routledge. 297–322.

Borgatti, S. P. & Cross, R. (2003) A relational view of information seeking and learning in social networks, *Management Science*, 49(4), 432–445.

Bradford, S. B. & Kozlowski, S. W. J. (2002) A typology of virtual teams: implications for effective leadership, *Group Organization Management*, 27, 14–49.

Burdick, D. (2009) *The Huffington Post*. Top 10 Greenwashing Companies In America. Retrieved 2 October 2015, from www.huffingtonpost.com/2009/04/03/top-10-greenwashing-compa_n_182724.html

Burt, R. S. (1992) *Structural Holes*, Boston, MA: Harvard University Press.

Crisp, C. B. & Jarvenpaa, S. L., (2013) Swift trust in global virtual teams trusting beliefs and normative actions, *Journal of Personnel Psychology*, 12(1), 45–56.

DeFillippi, R. & Arthur, M. (1994) The boundaryless career: a competency-based perspective, *Journal Of Organizational Behavior*, 15(4), 307–324.

Dubrin, A. (2001) *Leadership: Research Findings, Practice and Skills*. Boston, MA: Houghton Mifflin.

Eby, L. T., M. Butts & A. Lockwood (2003) Predictors of success in the era of boundaryless careers, *Journal of Organizational Behavior*, 24(6), 689–708.

Fagiano, D. (1997) Managers vs. leaders: a corporate fable, *Management Review*, 10: 5–6.

Gibbons, G. E., Hisrich, R. D., DaSilva, C. M. (2014) *Entrepreneurial Finance: A Global Perspective*. Los Angeles, CA: Sage.

Greenpeace USA (2013) Greenpeace Greenwash Criteria. Retrieved 2 October 2015, from www.stopgreenwash.org/

Hall, D. T. (1976) *Careers in Organizations*, Pacific Palisades, CA: Goodyear.

Hisrich, R. D. (2012) *International Entrepreneurship: Starting, Developing, and Managing a Global Venture*. Los Angeles, CA: Sage.

Inkson, K. & Arthur, M. (2001) How to be a successful career capitalist, *Organizational Dynamics*, 30(1), 48–58.

Jarvenpaa, S. L., Shaw, T. R. & Staples, D. (2004) Toward contextualized theories of trust: the role of trust in global virtual teams, *Information Systems Research*, 15(3), 250–264.

Jones, C. & DeFillippi, R. (1996) Back to the future in film: combining industry and self knowledge to meet the career challenges of the 21st century, *Academy of Management Executive*, 10(4), 89–104.

Jones, C. & Lichtenstein, B. (2000) The 'architecture' of careers: how career competencies reveal firm dominant logic in professional services. In M. A. Peiperl, M. B. Arthur, R. Coffee & T. Morris (Eds), *Career Frontiers: New Conceptions of Working Lives*, Oxford: Oxford University Press. 153–176.

Jong, R., Schalk, R. & Curseu, P. L. (2008) Virtual communicating, conflicts and performance in teams, *Team Performance Management*, 14(7/8), 364–380.

Karliner, J. (2007) CorpWatch: a brief history of greenwash. Retrieved 2 October 2015, from www.corpwatch.org/article.php?id=243

Kirkman, B. L. & Mathieu, J. E. (2005) The dimensions and antecedents of team virtuality, *Journal of Management*, 31, 700–718.

Kristof, A. L., Brown, K. G., Sims, H. P., Smith, K. A. (1995) The virtual team: a case study and inductive model. In M. M. Beyerlein, D. A. Johnson & S. T. Beyerlein (Eds.) *Advances in Interdisciplinary Studies of Work Teams: Knowledge Work in Teams*, Vol. 2. Greenwich, CT: JAI Press, 229–253.

Kuratko, D. F. (2013) *Entrepreneurship: Theory, Process, and Practice*, Boston, MA: Cengage Learning.

Matlay, H. & Westhead, P. (2005) Virtual teams and the rise of e-entrepreneurship in Europe, *International Small Business Journal*, 23(3), 279–302.

Maznevski, M. S. & Chudoba, K. M. (2000) Bridging space over time: global virtual team dynamics and effectiveness, *Organizational Science*, 11(5), 473–492.

Mintzberg, H. (1998) Covert leadership: notes on managing professionals, *Harvard Business Review*, November–December, 140–147.

Montoya-Weiss, M. M., Massey, A. P., Song, M. (2001) Getting it together: temporal coordination and conflict management in global virtual teams, *Academy of Management Journal*, 44(6), 1251–1262.

Mulki, J., Bardhi, F., Lassk, F. & Nanavaty-Dahl, J. (2009) Set up remote workers to thrive, *Mitsloan Management Review*, 51(1) 63–69.

Nahapiet, J. & Ghoshal, S. (1998) Social capital, intellectual capital, and the organizational advantage, *Academy of Management Review*, 23(2), 242–266.

Oviatt, B. M., McDougall, P. P. & Loper, M. (1995) Global start-ups: entrepreneurs on a worldwide stage, *The Academy of Management Executive*, 9(2), 30–43.

Parker, H. & Arthur, M. B. (2000) Careers, organizing, and community. In M. A. Peiperl, M. B. Arthur, R. Coffee & T. Morris (Eds.), *Career Frontiers: New Conceptions of Working Lives*, Oxford: Oxford University Press.

PriceWaterhouseCoopers, (2000) Managing a virtual world: international non-standard assignments, *Policy and Practice*, Europe: PricewaterhouseCoopers.

Raider, H. J. & Burt, R. S. (1996) Boundaryless careers and social capital. In M. B. Arthur & D. M. Rousseau, (1996) *The Boundaryless Career: A New Employment Principle for a New Organizational Era*. Oxford: Oxford University Press. 187–200.

Reis, C. (2010) Sensemaking of managers' ethical work orientations, *Social Responsibility Journal*, 6(1), 143–155

Reis, C. (2016) Managers' remote work and expertise across cultures in small–medium companies, *Journal of Applied Management and Entrepreneurship* (in press).

Reis, C. & Baruch, Y. (Eds.) (2013) *Careers Without Borders: Critical Perspectives*, New York: Routledge. Chapter 1.

Sandberg, S. (2013) *Lean In*, New York: Random House.

World Bank (2013) World Development Report, Retrieved 2 October 2015, from http://siteresources.worldbank.org/EXTNWDR2013/Resources/8258024132095074719/8260293–1322665883147/WDR_2013_Report.pdf.

Zahra, S. A., Jennings, D. F. & Kuratko, D. F. (1999) The antecedents and consequences of firm-level entrepreneurship: the state of the field, *Entrepreneurship Theory and Practice*, 24(2), 45–66.

Zaleznik, A. (1977) Managers and leaders: are they different?, *Harvard Business Review*, May–June: 67–68.

Zigurs, I. (2003) Leadership in virtual teams: oxymoron or opportunity?, *Organizational Dynamics*, 31(4), 339–351.

6 The Family Work of Executives and Organizations

Introduction

This article reviews the family work of executives that continues to be produced indirectly for organizations. This topic is integrated in the field of careers; it goes beyond work–life balance and employee well-being company policies, and is usually considered part of daily life routines – trivial and normalized. It is integrated in the field of TM because this type of work is crucial for most organizations and it is mainly produced for people who work in organizations at the highest levels of management.

Before introducing the concept of family work, it is important to note that many societies currently recognize a broad range of definitions regarding the meaning of family. Fraenkel (1999), for example, argues that there is no single definition of 'family'; since families are becoming increasingly diverse,

> there are single career as well as dual career families, two parent as well as single parent families, 'intact' as well as blended families, married as well as unmarried cohabiting parents, heterosexual as well as same sex parents, single race as well as interracial families, two- as well as three-generational families.

Others (e.g., Norwood, 2012) assert an expanding notion of 'family', which includes different families than the usual heterosexual couples. Gender in the management field and careers has been ignored as a subject of family work produced for organizations, which are more concerned with women in powerful positions. For centuries, a few women have managed to achieve powerful professional positions, but this is not the reality for the majority of women in most societies (see Baruch and Reis, 2015). In reality, the institutional support and the inclusion of all participants in the organizational structure who work inside and outside organizations is an overlooked subject. For example, even diversity management concepts do not include the variety of family arrangements that relate to the contextual meaning of 'diversity management' (Syed and Ozbilgin, 2009), signifying that it 'is most likely to be realized in contexts in which there is multilevel structural and institutional support for the inclusion and participation of all individuals and groups' (2436).

First, this article discusses how organizational theories generally present family work. Second, it presents a theoretical framework for the family work produced for organizations and which organizations disregard. There now follows how critical perspectives view this subject, along with an analogy with Utopia.

Family Work in Organizational Studies

Classical organizational theories were constructed around the male model of the 'ideal worker', who is task-oriented, without feelings and emotions, and asexual, while working in business settings. Ideally, '[t]he model of men and the model of masculinity are precise, behavioural, controlled and instrumental' (Hearn and Parkin, 1987: 19).

Inspired primarily by Parsonian systems thinking, the 'functionalist paradigm' is the dominant approach in organization research. Parsons drew strong linkages between task divisions and maintenance: 'The nuclear family with a clear gender division of labour between the 'externally-orientated' male and the 'integrative' female is drawn as a paradigm case for application to groups and organisations' (33). This type of systems theory justified the role of women in a subordinate position.

Despite feminist criticism of this type of management research – which began in the 1960s – and the acceptance of gender issues as being important, as well as serious questions being asked by more and more scholars in organizational studies (e.g., Alvesson and Billing, 1997), the discussion of family work produced for organizations is still relatively limited. Some writers intentionally do not consider the work produced outside organizations as part of their academic field. For example, Gunz and Jalland (1996), in their study about careers and strategy, define careers in the sense of observable work (employment) histories over time, and argue that other aspects, such as work outside organizations, are in general subjective and belong to other academic fields.

Despite this, some authors show concern with modern forms of social domination in connection with organizational studies; they do not recognize it and they do not systematically analyze family work produced for organizations. Their discussion is only a reference to this existing work; therefore, they limit their understanding of family work in connection with organizations. There are several studies on gender and organization from different feminist perspectives (see the overview in Calas and Smirchich, 1996). Nevertheless, few authors systematically integrate family work as an important matter in organizations studies.

Among the many different feminist studies in organizations, Davies' (1996) work developed a deep knowledge regarding how the notions of professions and bureaucracies have emerged in organizations at the cost of gender and class oppression. The author explains these processes by referring to closure theory, and discusses why well-rewarded and high-status professions are male-dominated. Wajcman (1998) compares men and women in similar senior managerial positions in the workplace. She critically sums up the main limitation in her own study: 'even here, the organization of domestic life and the household division of labour has received scant attention' (138).

Some authors discuss family work and analyze the differences in the career development of women and men (e.g., Sekaran and Hall, 1989; Hakim, 2000), but again they do not offer an analysis of the significance of family work produced for an organization. The concept of family work is used in a fragmentary manner, mainly as a variable, but also as a preference and even as a stereotype.

Others have researched wives' work in connection to organizations (e.g., Pahl and Pahl, 1971; Kanter, 1977; Kanter, 1994) but neither of the studies see the importance of the gender hierarchy as structuring work and family relations. These authors' understanding of family work outside organizations ignores the importance of contextual gender and hierarchy as structuring both work and family relations.

Another attempt in organizational theories has been to try to connect, somehow, women's work and family work with theories of embodiment and monstrosity (e.g., Vachhani, 2009). However, these wishful research descriptions have no notion of how patriarchy has developed in societies, and they focus on heterosexual bodies as not fitting with the necessary pre-conditions of formal organizations (e.g., Cooper and Burrel, 1988; Chia, 1988).

In summary, most research in organizations studies does not analyze family work produced for organizations and/or the reasons for its continuity in connection with organizations.

The Work Produced by the Family for Organizations

Using the expression 'unspoken work' of Reis (2004), I developed the relevance of the concept of family work produced for organizations. This work is done in the private sphere of organizational managers, and it is unspoken work because it is not elaborated so as to be expressed into words. This happens because this work is natural and is produced in such a way that it is normalized, unquestionably trivial, and therefore not worth talking about (much less that it should deserve scientific attention). It is excluded from public discussions within organizations because is disagreeable and disturbs the established social order in which many people live. Nobel Prize economists (e.g., Becker, 1965; 1976; 1981) have ignored how this work is produced and the reasons for it.

However, Reis (2004) used a methodology called 'listening to the material life in discursive practices' (Reis, 2014) which focuses on the discursive practices of ideal material structures and how people live through them. It concentrates less on how certain individuals have overcome difficulties with creative ideas or seized opportunities for themselves (and only themselves) to escape the work produced by the family for organizations. It focuses on societies, people, organizations and careers. This methodology challenges neo-liberalist, essentialist and naturalistic accounts about differences in the work produced by families, and is primarily visible when families support their middle-class standard of living and social status.

Regarding the production of family work, Delphy and Leonard (1992), better than anybody else in their field, have clarified how generations of family relations became a unit of consumption, a unit of production, and a mode of the accumulation and circulation of property. It is through transmission within the family and the quality of consumption of family members that this theory conceptualizes the differences between family relations and labor market relations. They conceptualize their definition of 'family' as a social institution that pre-exists as a system in space and time with conditioned choices to set their own parameters: '[t]heir actions in relation to it are free only within a framework which ranges from social norms to coercive and penal controls' (265–6).

The authors differentiate very clearly between the market system and the family system. Such a difference is technically (for the purpose of analysis) important in this chapter because the labor market corresponds to organizations while family systems correspond to family work. Consequently, although the family has a hierarchical structure, there is no formal exchange in terms of resources and services; therefore, wageworkers cannot be compared with family workers because neither payment nor evaluation exists in the family. Family workers are not free, that is, they do not possess their own labor power. Family work responds to a hierarchy, which is both gendered and generational in time and circumstances.

Although it can be said that, today, there is no hierarchy in the family, and that we live in a relatively genderless society and free of structures (see Chapter 2), this theory claims that long-standing social and cultural acceptance of traditional authority handed down from the past remains relatively stable in many social contexts. Of course, if we think about the production of an individual who lives relatively independently from others and has no organizational work at higher management levels, their self-consumption may not have any of these characteristics. According to this theory, family work is seen in terms of three different layers: actual family work, household work and housework.

- Family work: All the work done in the family is unpaid work if done by dependents in a kinship or marital relationship who feel that they are 'obliged' to do this work. Family work is remunerated through the leader[1] of the family.
- Household work: Includes housework, and covers emotional and sexual servicing, and procreative work. It also comprehends the production of goods and services which are not for the household's own consumption but rather for exchange on the market.

- Housework: Contemporary work, which includes the day-to-day tasks necessary to run the family.

It is possible that families do not have any housework to do in certain contexts or circumstances where 'servants' can be hired but still have to be managed. However, because of the belief that there is an obligation to support the family, servants are paid while the family serves the production of an organization (e.g., wealthy royal families).

Under many circumstances, family tasks can be regarded as normal, natural or trivialized, but definitely as a good thing for the family. Sometimes, these tasks are valued with 'love', but this is not reliable and can be subjective or without any concrete value. Since family work is conceptualized in this way, the work done in a hierarchical position for the family may not be recognized as having economic or monetary value. Often, the providers of this labor are usually not in control or not even aware of the use of their labor. The more privileges that such family laborers receive through the family, the less aware they are of this work and the more they disregard their dependency on the family and how their work is used by others in organizations.

Understanding the Family Work Produced for Organizations

This section presents two examples to explain the analysis of family work produced for organizations (for a more complete understanding, see Reis, 2004). The accounts come from a study about 'men managers', and they explain the importance of family work in their view. This chapter is not exploring male prejudices but rather showing a dominant reality that exists in our society and which can be listened to through the use of a specific methodology, as it is 'the material life of discursive practices' (see Reis, 2014, for the methodological details). The following account shows the importance of the *housework* (emphasis added) done by in-laws.

> [I]f me and my wife have a seminar or we have to go to a foreign country for a few days, it is never a problem and we always go because my father-in-law would take care […], when the children were small my mother-in-law lived near us. Sometimes, my mother also went to pick up the children from the kindergarten. We were lucky and we never had any problems in that respect. I was always lucky in having my parents-in-law to help, and I must tell you that my mother-in-law left her job to take care of my life and the life of my wife. My youngest son had problems in the kindergarten and she took care of him.
>
> Data reproduced from Reis, 2004

Most families need to go through these same day-to-day tasks which are essential to maintaining their well-being, education and health, etc. Indeed, this is the case with this family as well, and many would consider the work trivial. Since the concept of housework includes day-to-day tasks necessary to run the family, the producers of this labor expect some sort of exchange (e.g., love, caring for them when they become older or sick, etc.). Nonetheless, there is no guarantee that this exchange will occur since they are not in control of the effects and rewards of how their own labor is reproduced in freeing this couple to work for their organization (specified here as 'housework').

The second account explains the importance of the *household work* (emphasis added), which is part of family work.

> Always, and at any time, the wife may be called to be the hostess of my German colleagues or in any other country, when they come to visit with their wives, and normally they get together. In that sense, my wife has truly been a good hostess, and that I have at home – and that is extremely important [...] – good social conversation, a warm welcome, good communication.
>
> Data reproduced from Reis, 2004

This account explains household work done through socializing with people during business events by being a skillful communicator, entertaining others, being funny and supportive, managing to have good looks, etc. *From a critical perspective, these services are directly producing useful resources for the head of the household and indirectly so for organizations.*

Implications

Is this process of family work produced for organizations a matter of exploitation on the part of organizations? Although this process can be seen as positive, a critical theoretical analysis, as proposed in this article, shows that this is a matter of exploitation (see Chapters 8 and 10 of Reis, 2004). There are, obviously, those who believe that hierarchical family work produced for organizations is a very good thing. It may indeed be regarded as a wonderful domestic enterprise if there is loyalty among family members and acceptance of inequality over monetary control and the quality of consumption (e.g., usually the male head of the family drives the big, expensive car) and between generations and family members. This is true with some privileged families also whose members benefit more from the family than from a paid position of their own in the labor market. They may need to maintain their relationship with each other in order to obtain sufficient capital to maintain a certain high living-standard. When one family member has access to privileges, other family members may derive benefits from it as well.

Patriarchy is associated with protection, stability and the resource maintenance of family members. There is nothing 'bad' here if the head of the family is capable of sustaining and managing the family. However, this order may be reversed if a family member rebels or causes severe conflict within the family. Some contexts are governed by several families whose privileges are only available to some and not to the majority of the population.

From a critical perspective, family work has an impact on individuals at the level of their independency, their autonomy and the quality of their consumption. Moreover, there is no guarantee that family members will receive anything in any form (e.g., love, money, respect, etc.) for the work they have produced within the family. If family members are dependent upon the quality of consumption and the transmission in the family that maintains their social status and standard of living, it is possible that there will be disruption.

For example, some individuals are dependent upon family work and, at the same time, have well-paid jobs, could be financially independent, and have an accepted role in public life, yet they continue to maintain their dependency within their families and to provide family work. Why do they this work for the family? Family members believe in exchange based on 'love' and protection from other family members. Reis (2004, Chapter 8) demystified the notion that wives' work for their husbands is not 'team work', yet wives are part of the system of family work subject to the hierarchy of gender, with a subordinate status.

This becomes significantly more evident when married women try to resist the demands of their partners (male managers in higher positions in organizations) over the long-term. They may face serious material and social costs. They are penalized in their relationships with other people and they are demoted to a lower social status; ultimately, they are relegated to a lower standard of living. Pahl (1989) suggests that,

> [d]ivorce reveals the reality which lies behind the assumption that couples pool their resources. A growing body of research has shown that when marriages end women and children typically receive a meagre share of the husbands' resources, if they receive anything at all. (8)

In divorces, when it is said that the wife receives 50 percent of the family resources, many heads of family when they have access to powerful lawyers instead give their wives an agreement whereby the women end up with significantly less than their deserved share of the family resources. Even when wives have a certain level of financial independence, sometimes they prefer to maintain their marriages because they fear social resistance and emotional oppression by their friends and families, as well as by their superiors and colleagues in the workplace. Moreover, material wealth and the social inclusion of their children may be at stake. Ultimately, they fear poverty, the loss of social acceptance and increased isolation.

The material advantages gained through marriage (particularly a high standard of living) represent an important aspect of the problem; indeed, individual women may be better off inside, rather than outside, of marriage.

These theoretical statements may seem outdated but, if the reader were to look around they might observe how the workers of certain private organizations (including private universities in the USA) manage their wives' work for their own careers. These wives have to be invited to all public events and through a discourse they integrate them in their professional lives – they are a family. When there is a documentary about them in newspapers, these wives often appear as decorators of their husbands' offices in the organizations they work for, or as members of the board of certain charities, and so on.

Conclusion

Organizations, by encouraging the family responsibilities of their employees, contribute to the exploitation of family work. The ideology of having a family and a 'good solid marriage', favored by employers, makes employees feel responsible for their families. Employers regard it as an issue related to work performance, commitment to the job, and loyalty to the company. They expect employees, at higher levels in particular, to be fully engaged with and highly committed to their jobs. It is then less necessary and, therefore, less cost-intensive to control them. *Although organizations clearly maintain the production of family work, employers are not interested in the conditions of economic dependency or social isolation under which family work is provided.*

Some authors in organizational studies (e.g., Bloomfield and Vurdubakis, 1999) have opened up the discussion of the unnoticed, and they claim to distinguish what happens inside and outside organizations; however, the conditions under which family work is produced and the consequences for individual members continue to be ignored in this field.

The heads of families strengthen companies' family ideologies by making their own lives dependent upon an employer who can meet their specific needs for a high standard of living, high social status and strong masculine values and symbols (e.g., company car, networks, etc.). It is a process of employees and their families reproducing social structures and organizations supporting this via their human resources, management strategies and practices.

Although it has been claimed that societies today have become more individualized, with people managing their own lives and work, in times of crises when good employment is difficult to obtain, individuals – particularly young people – become less autonomous and more dependent upon their families. *The goal of this chapter has been to review the understanding of how family work continues to be produced indirectly for organizations, mainly through executives' work, and how it has been maintained in today's organizations.*

Future research could investigate and compare organizations regarding the exploration of the work produced indirectly by families mainly through executives' work.

From a critical perspective, this is a reflection upon the work produced by the family and how individuals can be autonomous from the reliance on various forms of subordination, inequality and various relations of social power. Obviously, executives' family members who engage in this work are not autonomous, and so neither is the executive. Are these executive careers useful? They are responsible for each other, which can be a wonderful thing, but it is not in the conditions of their own choosing. It is a double-edged and unspoken organizational requirement which was conceptualized as 'unspoken work' by Reis (2004). Regarding TM, and for the executives who perform well in their careers and at the same time have the benefit of the work produced by the family, they certainly have an edge over those executives who do not have any family work produced for them and who cannot buy it in the form of services (without genuine love and reliability).

Although some may think that, today, we live in a genderless society – that is, in 2015 people saw on TV the announcement of the new royal baby born in the UK. At the top of a tower in London, a script was displaying 'It's a girl'. As Julia Kristeva said in the 1970s, women as such do not exist – rather they are in the process of becoming. It is right at the moment when the baby is born that the gender process starts, as the baby is identified and desired as a 'female'. Although this is a theoretical perspective, one might expect that these things are outdated, and that it should not really matter as to the sex of a baby. The issue is that such esteemed families are regarded as examples for most middle- and working-class people in the world – these people enjoy or are followers of such gendered behaviors. If we think back to Utopia, gender behaviors exist and are clearly differentiated and submitted to a social order of normalization as is the case for most of our societies today. It is unremarkable how overlooked family work (and this relates not only to gender or women issues) continues to be as a part of an organized social order, careers and TM.

Note

1 In most contexts, the man is the head of the household. Family work can be indirectly exploited through the leader of the family by organizations.

References

Alvesson, M. & Billing, Y. D. (1997) *Understanding Gender and Organizations.* London, Thousand Oaks, New Delhi: Sage Publications.

Bloomfield, B. & Vurdubakis, T. (1999) The outer limits: actor networks and the writing of displacement, *Organization* 6(4): 625–647

Baruch, Y. & Reis, C. (2015) Global career challenges for women crossing international borders. In A. Broadbridge & S. L. Fielden, (Eds.), *Handbook of Gendered Careers in Management: Getting In, Getting On, Getting Out.* Cheltenham, UK; Northampton, MA, USA: Edward Elgar.

Becker, G. S. (1965) A theory of allocation of time, *Economic Journal*, 75, 493–517.

Becker, G. S. (1976) *The Economic Approach to Human Behavior.* Chicago, IL: University of Chicago Press.

Becker, G. S. (1981) *A Treatise on the Family.* Cambridge, MA: Harvard University Press.

Calas, M. & Smirchich, L. (1996) From 'the women's' point of view: feminist approaches to organisation studies. In S. R. Clegg, C. Hardy, & W. Nord (Eds.), *Handbook of Organization Studies.* London, Thousand Oaks, New Delhi: Sage. 218–258.

Chia, R. (1988) Introduction: exploring the expanded realm in technology, organizations and modernity. In R. Chia (Ed.) *Organized Worlds: Explorations in Technology and Organization with Robert Cooper.* London: Routledge. 1–19.

Collinson, D. L. & Hearn, J. (Eds.) (1996) *Men as Managers, Managers as Men: Critical Perspectives on Men, Masculinities and Managements.* London: Sage Publications.

Cooper, R. & Burrell, G. (1988) Modernism, post modernism and organizational analysis: an introduction, *Organization Studies*, 9(19), 91–112.

Davies, C. (1996) The sociology of professions and the profession of gender, *Sociology*, 30(4) 661–678.

Delphy, C. & Leonard, D. (1992) *Familiar exploitation: a new analysis of marriage in the contemporary society.* Cambridge, MA: Cambridge Center.

du Gay, P. (1994) Colossal immodesties and hopeful monsters: pluralism and organizational conduct, *Organization*, 1(81), 125–148.

Fraenkel, P. (1999) All about fathers, *Child Study Center Newsletter*, 4(2).

Grey, C. (1994) Career as a project of the self and labour process discipline, *Sociology*, 28(2), 479–497.

Gunz, H. P. & Jalland, M. R. (1996) Managerial careers and business strategies, *Journal Academy Managerial Review*, 21(3), 718–756.

Hakim, C. (2000) *Work–Lifestyle Choices in the 21st Century: Preference Theory.* Oxford: Oxford University Press.

Hearn, J. & Parkin, W. (1987) *'Sex' at 'Work': The Power and Paradox of Organisation Sexuality.* Brighton: Wheatsheaf Books.

Kanter, R. M. (1977) *Men and Women of the Corporation.* New York: Basic Books.

Law, J. (1991) *A Sociology of Monsters: Essays on Power, Technology and Domination.* London: Routledge.

Munro, R. (2001) Calling for accounts: numbers, monsters and membership, *Sociological Review*, 49(4), 473–473.

Norwood, K. (2012) Transitioning meanings? Family members' communicative struggles surrounding transgender identity, *Journal of Family Communication*, 12(1), 75–92.

Oakley, A. (2005) *The Ann Oakley Reader: Gender, Women and Social Science.* Bristol: Policy Press.

Pahl, J. (1989) *Money and Marriage.* Basingstoke: Macmillan.

Pahl, J. M. & Pahl, R. E. (1971) *Managers and their Wives: A Study of Career and Family Relationships in the Middle Class.* Harmondsworth: Penguin Books.

Parker, M. (2000) Manufacturing bodies: flesh, organization, cyborgs. In J. Hassard, R. Holliday & H. Willmott (Eds) *Body and Organization.* London: Sage. 71–86.

Reis, C. (2004) *Men Working as Managers in a European Multinational Company*, München; Mering: Rainer Hampp Verlag.

Reis, C. (2014) Listening to the material life in discursive practices, *Tamara Journal for Critical Organizational Inquirer*, 12(2), 1–6.

Reis, C. & Baruch, Y. (Eds.) (2013) *Careers without Borders: Critical Perspectives*, New York: Routledge.

Sekaran, U. & Hall, T. D. (1989) A synchronism in dual-career and family linkages. In M. B. Arthur, D. T. Hall, & B. S. Lawrence (Eds.), *Handbook of Career Theory.* Cambridge: Cambridge University Press.

Shildrick, M. (2002) *Embodying the Monster: Encounters with the Vulnerable Self.* London: Sage.

Syed, J. & Ozbilgin, M. (2009) A relational framework for international transfer of diversity management practices, *The International Journal of Human Resource Management*, 20(12), 2435–2453.

Vachhani, S. (2009) Vagina dentate and the demonological body: explorations of the feminine demon in organisation. In A. Pullen & C. Rhodes (Eds) *Bits of Organization* Malmo, Sweden: Liber.

Wajcman, J. (1998) *Managing like a Man: Women and Men in Corporate Management*, Pennsylvania: The Pennsylvania State University Press.

7 Socially Responsible Executives

Introduction

Senior executives' careers theories often focus upon explaining CEO succession (e.g., Marcel and Cowen, 2014) or upon whether age matters in continuing as an executive in the same organization. Ward et al. (1995) found that age matters and that older CEOs were less likely to obtain other active executive positions, and that instead they would be in advisory roles. In addition, research of CEOs' careers histories reveals that their career moves outside an organization are negatively related to career rewards (e.g., Kakarika, 2009). In other words, CEOs' career moves within the same organization have more potential for the achievement of rewards rather than attempting a personal career strategy with career moves across different employers. Hamori and Koyuncu (2011) reinforce this argument where senior executives take international assignments other than from their current employer and when taking international assignments at later stages of their careers – it damages their career advancement.

Usually, senior executives following retirement will engage in a post-corporate career, the concept of which was developed first by Peiperl and Baruch (1997). The authors identified post-corporate careerists as being 'self-directed, tak[ing] responsibility for their own career management, perceive[ing] a variety of career of career options, and [being] willing to cross multiple boundaries to fulfil their needs for intrinsic job satisfaction as well as financial rewards' (Sullivan and Baruch, 2009: 1555). The variety of their alternative employment arrangements includes independent contractors, temporary workers and working for small firms that provide services to large organizations (Sullivan and Baruch, 2009). Senior executives' widely held assumptions on the engagement of a post-corporate career following retirement will be examined in this paper along with the concept of the 'boundaryless' career. There is also biographical data showing that executives near retirement aim to continue their careers as executives.

Mr. Ballmer says he is weighing casual offers as varied as university teaching and coaching his youngest son's high-school basketball team. He plans no big decisions for at least six months – except that he won't run another big company. He says he's open to remaining a Microsoft director.

Langley, 2013, in the Wall Street Journal

The notion of a 'boundaryless' career was developed by Arthur and Rousseau (1996), whereby individuals are independent of traditional career arrangements and are free to work with different employers (DeFillippi and Arthur, 1996), which opens a new agenda for senior executives who aim to be executives in more than one organization. Several scholars have studied the concept of the boundaryless career (Baruch, 2004; Sullivan, 1999; Marler et al., 2002; Peiperl and Estrin, 2000; Valcour and Tolbert, 2003; Kirchmeyer, 2002; Ibarra, 2003), and it has been studied cross-nationally (e.g., Segers et al., 2008), including within retirement (e.g., Wang et al., 2009), and among other topics such as expatriate assignments, mentoring, learning and development. The boundaryless career has been critically reviewed and examined by Sullivan and Baruch (2009). In this respect, Sullivan and Baruch (2009) review of the protean concept suggested that more research is needed on the protean career orientations within different cultures. However, little theoretical attention has been paid to understanding why executives near retirement would aim to engage in a boundaryless career as executives in other organizations. To some people, the idea that senior executives near the age of retirement would aim for a second chance as an executive in another organization seems silly, but empirical observations suggests the opposite.

However, Baruch and Reis (2015) argue that the recent discourse in the career studies literature suggests that careers have become more boundaryless and more global. The scope of these phenomena and the possible association between them remains unclear. The authors challenged individuals and organizations to delve into how individuals interpret their way out of their contextual systems in order to engage in global careers, and how different contextual aspects influence the desire for and the perception of global careers.

TM and career development is lacking for older employees (Van Rooij, 2012), and this chapter aims to fill a further theoretical void by exploring a broad range of reasons for executives to engage in a second career as executives.

To facilitate such a research agenda, this paper offers several theoretical propositions about the factors that may affect the degree to which senior executives will consider when they identify new career opportunities to work for more than one organization. As a result, this chapter makes two important contributions to the literature on careers and TM for senior executives. First, it focuses on important aspects of senior executives career aims in pursuing their multiple roles as executives which have received little attention in the literature. Second, it helps to move this literature in more theoretically oriented directions by offering a set of different propositions which relates to globalization and social responsibility, and which has implications for the boundaryless careers of senior executives' late lives.

Senior Executives' Aims

In this section, I discuss important aspects of senior executives' career aims that may motivate them to increase their contribution as executives to more than one organization. Why would senior executives engage in a boundaryless career for more than one organization later on in their lives?

One way of analyzing executives' decisions to engage in a boundaryless career as an executive late in life is through the three dimensions of the individual intelligent career/capital framework. These dimensions can be summarized in terms of knowing-why, knowing-how and knowing-whom (DeFillippi and Arthur, 1994; Eby et al., 2003; Inkson and Arthur, 2001). The *knowing-why career capital dimension* concentrates mainly on the identification with self-purpose through work. This dimension views the individual's identity's detachment from employers and opens a new outlet for individual career experiences (Arthur et al., 1999; Eby et al., 2003). Issues such as motivation and a personal sense of worth are connected with self-confidence in leading a desired career (Inkson and Arthur, 2001; Jones and Lichtenstein, 2000). The search for self-fulfillment of the knowing-why dimension of career capital is also in line with the concept of the internal career issues of the protean career (Hall, 1976). In this sense, this career capital dimension is necessary to engage in a boundaryless career late in life.

Proposition 1: *Senior executives identify their own self-purpose through work, which may lead to engagement in a boundaryless career late in life.*

Another career capital dimension is that of *knowing-how*, which focuses mainly on the individual skills and knowledge required to perform up to organizational standards (DeFillippi and Arthur, 1994). For the boundaryless careers of senior executives, the emphasis is on the acquisition of their own transferable skills, which can be used across organizations (Eby et al., 2003).

Proposition 2: *Senior executives can transfer their skills across organizations, which enables their boundaryless careers.*

The *knowing-whom career capital dimension* refers to all professional and personal career-relevant networks and contacts (DeFillippi and Arthur, 1994; Parker and Arthur, 2000; Borgatti and Cross, 2003). It is related to the literature on social capital (Raider and Burt, 1996), referring to assets that can be developed through a network of relationships useful to individual career development (Jones and DeFillippi, 1996; Nahapiet and Ghoshal, 1998; Adler and Kwon, 2002). 'Social capital' refers to the benefits derived from linking people or social units that would otherwise not be connected (Burt, 1992). Research shows that personal and professional contacts give individuals an advantage in relation to information and career opportunities (e.g., Burt, 1992; Granovetter, 1973), and these advantages consist in accessing unique information in advance, and a way of getting supportive referrals by attracting connections and prestige (Burt, 1992), which is relevant to enable the boundaryless careers of senior executives late in life.

Proposition 3: *Senior executives may have advantages in accessing unique information across organizations which will enable their boundaryless careers.*

Another interesting tool of analysis of senior executives' aims is through that of systems skills from Bird and Osland (2004). Systems skills present a progressive pyramid via blocks of competencies whereby, at the top of the pyramid, is the skill of mastering across different businesses, which implies the engagement in ethical decisions.

Ethical decisions are the highest challenge in the pyramid proposed by Bird and Osland (2004) and, according to Reis (2008), executives have different ethical orientations. Some executives may experience difficulties in identifying whether they need to make an ethical decision or not in unexpected situations. Most executives cannot engage in the process of making ethical decisions since they have personal conflicts when they face controversy or else are not even aware that they have to resolve an ethical problem. Ethical issues are usually publicly known and easy to identify, while ethical dilemmas are controversial and not publicly validated as an ethical issue. Executives' self-identities are also reflected in their recognition of ethical problems and decision-making (Reis, 2010), and these actions reveal their career aims.

Proposition 4: *Executives who have an ethical orientation capable of identifying ethical dilemmas beyond ethical issues are most likely to aim for a boundaryless career late in life.*

Nonetheless, is it feasible to have more than one senior role as an executive across organizations? The next section offers a theoretical framework within a discussion of social responsibility issues in organizations that may or may not enable the boundaryless careers of senior executives.

Socially Responsible Organizations

Why do some senior executives engage in boundaryless careers while others do not? Is it purely dependent upon a personal choice, or is there something more to it? Put in slightly different terms, under what conditions are senior executives more likely to engage in a boundaryless career? One idea to answer these questions would be to involve the literature on social responsibility, which is concerned with the variations in corporate behavior across different cultures and economic environments. As discussed in the previous section, senior executives' ethical identity is important and relates to their organizational freedom in ethical decision-making. Most likely, they will choose sustainable organizations where there is an appeal to contribute both to other sustainable organizations, with their skills and knowledge, and also to the well-being of societies and future generations. The focus on corporate social responsibility engages managers in making effective use of their talents (Tymon et al., 2010; Vaiman et al., 2012; Al Ariss et al., 2014).

Beginning with the stakeholder theory within a social responsibility perspective, researchers recognize that the way in which corporations treat their stakeholders depends upon the organizations within which they operate (e.g., Fligstein and Freeland, 1995; Hall and Soskice, 2001). In the same way, senior executives will recognize their opportunities as executives across organizations by the way in which these organizations treat their stakeholders. First, it is necessary to define what is meant by stakeholder theory in the context of executives' boundaryless careers. Following the social responsibility literature, stakeholders are 'individuals or groups with which the corporation interacts [and] who have a stake or a vested interest in it' (Carroll and Buchholtz, 2000: 21). Stakeholders usually include employees, consumers, suppliers and local communities, and they will influence the opportunities for senior executives in a second role as executives if they see that they are bringing an improvement to themselves through the work they will do in the organization. Stakeholder theory is important because, according to Campbell (2007), corporations act in socially responsible ways if they do two things. First, they must not perceptively do anything that could harm their stakeholders and, second, if corporations do cause harm to their stakeholders, they must then rectify this as soon as it is discovered and brought to their attention.

Stakeholder theorists have been trying to provide frameworks by which an organization can be identified as socially responsible. Clarkson (1995) suggests that a stakeholder is relevant if they have invested something in the organization and are therefore subject to risk in relation to that organization's activities. Others have developed a framework for identifying and ranking stakeholders in terms of their power, legitimacy and urgency (Mitchell, Agle and Wood, 1997). It is also argued that involuntary stakeholders, such as individuals, communities, ecological environments and future generations, do not choose to deal with the organization, and therefore may need some form of protection that may be provided through government legislation or regulation. However, other more specific interest groups may be relevant for certain industries due to the nature of the industry or the specific activities of the organization: 'Utility industries have been regulated by a regulator since privatization and thus the regulator is a stakeholder of these organizations' (Crowther and Aras, 2008: 33).

Taking into account the variations among stakeholder theories, senior executives may be in a position to manage specific interest groups of stakeholders due to their prestige and legitimacy gained during the course of their careers in certain industries.

Proposition 5: *Senior executives know how to manage specific groups of stakeholders in the industries which are associated with their careers and talents and which may enable their boundaryless careers.*

These insights can help move the analysis of the boundaryless career of senior executives in a more theoretically oriented direction, since stakeholder theory is an important decision tool for them to know whether there is a serious opportunity in those organizations to have a second role as an executive.

There are other important social responsibility issues which can be assessed by senior executives when choosing whether or not to engage in a boundaryless career. Other issues include bad practices and threats to the public. Assuming that corporations try to act in responsible ways while maximizing profit and shareholder value, senior executives need to go beyond these activities and check whether there are serious threats related to social responsibility issues or practices. Regarding the aims of senior executives in having a boundaryless career, these issues have to be considered since they may run the risk of being given a position that has been left behind by incompetent management. The new management may not be able to resolve the threats for which they are hired given the purpose of a 'green wash' or the 'pretense of socially responsible behavior through artful reporting' (Crowther and Aras, 2008: 20).

Proposition 6: *Senior executives may need to investigate organizational malpractices before accepting to work for another organization and engaging in a boundaryless career.*

It is important for senior executives to have knowledge about the meaning and practices of sustainable organizations. For example, the 'triple bottom line', which descends from the starting point on sustainable corporate activity or the Brundtland Report, reviews three aspects of performance which can be influential in senior executives' decisions as regards the engagement of a boundaryless career.

The triple bottom line focuses on aspects of performance which are economic, social and environmental. Beginning with the economic aspects of this legacy, three main economic conditions can be taken into account by senior executives when deciding whether to engage in a boundaryless career: financial performance, intense competition, and no competition.

Organizations tend to engage in less socially responsible behavior when financial performance is weak (e.g., Margolis and Walsh, 2001; Orlitsky et al., 2003). The argument is based on the lack of resources theory (Waddock and Graves, 1997), which states that firms with fewer resources are less profitable and it is assumed that these spend less in socially responsible activities and take fewer risks regarding shareholder value.

Assuming that these organizations ignore stakeholders, as defined here, and act only in their self-interest when the economic environment is not healthy (e.g., high inflation, low-productivity growth, weak consumer confidence, no short-term profit expectancy), organizations may tend to be less socially responsible.

Proposition 7: *Senior executives will be less likely to accept a position in an organization with weak financial performance due to the risk of engaging in a less socially responsible executive role for their boundaryless careers.*

In intensely competitive economic environments, organizations may tend to save money by avoiding risk for shareholders, surviving with minimum profits and disregarding socially responsible activities. These assumptions are based on historical periods of very intense competition which view socially irresponsible activities in organizations (Kolko, 1963; McCraw, 1984; Schneiberg, 1999; Weinstein, 1968). However, compromising the trust of the suppliers and customers of the organization may be even more risky in the long term, since they can take their business elsewhere. In this sense, when organizational survival is not at stake, the administration becomes more concerned with preserving the reputation of a sustainable business.

Proposition 8: *Senior executives will be less likely to accept a position in an organization with intense competition due to the risk of engaging in a less socially responsible executive role.*

The other situation is when organizations have little competition and do not care for socially responsible issues or their reputation. Although organizations should recognize that they do not need to engage in socially irresponsible activities in order to be competitive under such conditions, stakeholders have very few choices or alternatives and is too risky to assume negotiations with such organizations operating in such economic conditions.

Proposition 9: *Senior executives will be less likely to accept a position in an organization if there is too little competition, which will block their boundaryless careers.*

The two other aspects of the triple bottom line are the social and the environmental, and these have been challenged by a model with four other factors important for sustainable development as proposed by Aras and Crowther (2007). This model is open to different interpretations and can be adapted to the boundaryless career of senior executives. The balance between these last four sustainable aspects may enable senior executives to take a decision to engage in boundaryless careers as executives.

The first aspect is financial, which relates to the economic aspect of the triple bottom line model. This aspect reinforces how important the financial aspect is in relation to the internal focus of the organization within a short-term focus. Since this analytical aspect can be observed within a short-term framework, it enables senior executives to make a decision about their boundaryless careers.

The second aspect concerns the organizational culture, which can be defined in many ways (e.g., Schein, 1996). In the context of a boundaryless career for senior executives, it may be important to work for an organization where individual spiritual and cultural values are aligned with corporate and societal values. It promotes all other aspects of the corporate sustainability model and individual careers for a common good.

The third aspect maps onto the conservation of the environment, which may be essential to senior managers when taking a decision as to whether to engage in a boundaryless career. The options for a sustainable environment are important aspects to maintain and create for the future of generations to come.

The fourth aspect is societal influence, and it is very important for senior managers to manage community activities (such as social justice, continuity of education, the elimination of different forms of poverty, etc.) which are not necessarily only promoted by non-profit but also profit organizations.

Proposition 10: *Senior executives will more likely to accept a position in a sustainable organization which meets the triple bottom line, which will enable their boundaryless careers.*

Cross-cultural Experiences and Skills

Other issues that can be relevant for senior executives in engaging in a boundaryless career are their own cross-cultural experiences and global skills. Several authors have studied the characteristics and orientations of global executives' careers (e.g., Thomas and Osland, 2004; Peirperl and Jonsen, 2007; Dickmann and Baruch, 2010). In the context of opportunities that may enable the boundaryless career of senior executives, these may be available in global organizations. Opportunities for senior executives to engage in a global boundaryless career with multiple roles may have been released by global economies. A boundaryless career can be global, and global careers occur 'when part of that sequence takes place in more than one country' (Dickmann and Baruch, 2011: 7). Further, global careers may come in various types and forms, with several dimensions helping to make distinctions across different types of global careers (Baruch, et al., 2013).

Senior executives can engage in another organization as executives through a global assignment and where their experience as executives in other countries may be needed as decision–makers. As discussed in previous sections, the importance of managing community activities (such as social justice, continuity of education, the elimination of different forms of poverty, etc.) at the global level may enable a boundaryless career that has global characteristics. The management of community activities side by side with a global and profitable business implies ethical decisions, which are the highest challenge in the pyramid proposed by Bird and Osland (2004).

Proposition 11: *Senior executives may experience a global assignment which enables their boundaryless careers with global characteristics.*

Another opportunity that senior executives may consider relates to not-for-profit organizations. Here, there is no profit motive and decisions must be taken according to non-financial measures. The motivation of senior executives to engage in this kind of organization may be rewarding if, for example, their prestige in the business they used to manage pertains to lead stakeholders and fund-raising where competition is strong.

Proposition 12: *Senior executives may experience a boundaryless career in non-profit organizations.*

The next paragraph will discuss the implications of this theoretical framework, future research, as well as offering a conclusion within the framework of critical perspectives and Utopian way of life.

Implications and Conclusion

Socially responsible executives' careers and TM integrate a theoretical framework which is ideal but also feasible and necessary in our societies and organizations. The boundaryless careers of senior executives are useful careers.

From a critical perspective, and if the proposed theoretical conditions are met, senior executives can be an example of autonomous individuals with the ability to free themselves from reliance on some forms of subordination (e.g., to be dependent on the rules, values, strategies of one organization, particularly regarding careers and TM). If they perceive inequality and unfair relations of power, they may have the power and freedom to raise their voice against such practices and organizational ideas which other managers – who work for only one organization – are unable to do for fear of losing their jobs or else ideological involvement (e.g., they cannot see other ways of managing people).

Therefore, they have the openness to interconnect with other people in a way that allows them to feel responsible for others. Obviously, the practice of this ideal altruism of senior executives later in life depends upon their personality, upbringing, background and intercultural experiences as well as other factors as mentioned in this book. Future research could test whether senior executives could see themselves as integrated in a second career as executives as proposed by this theoretical framework.

In this chapter, I concentrated on senior executives because they are often regarded as leaders and an example for society as to how organizations should be managed, and they direct the organizational behavioral conduct of people even if this is not noticed by many. It is obvious that this theoretical framework could be applied to other professions, such as medical doctors, judges, chartered accountants, etc. For example, academics are believed to be highly responsible individuals because they teach others. However, people who live in an academic environment have often found the opposite. It is common to find dishonesty among academic colleagues, and a grapevine of false statements to gain power and advantages over others.

In summary, what does this chapter on careers and TM about socially responsible executives (which could be applied to other professions) share with *Utopia*. What can we learn from the Utopian when we live in an uncertain and global economy?

Assuming this theoretical framework, socially responsible executives are teachers of future generations. As in Utopia, knowledge is exchanged between those who have already been in the field and those who have such knowledge as to have the responsibility to teach other members of other families. In Utopia, information is simple and not hidden, as it should be with the ideal careers and TM teaching processes of socially responsible senior executives.

Regarding symbolism, Utopians accept their symbols of power and differentiation, in opposition to critical perspectives which aim to diminish and challenge the effects of patriarchal societies and differentiation in inequality and power. Utopians feel protected and united behind their buildings, towers and forts, and they never challenge patriarchy and the usefulness of their careers or talents.

Responsible senior executives' careers, as proposed in this chapter, can be a way to equilibrate the usefulness of careers or talents. Senior executives should not use forms of differentiation and dominance, because it is assumed that they are free of the ideologies and strategies of any one organization. However, responsible senior executives are not free from ideological structures shared by societies and other organizations. Gender divisions are the most impregnated, invisible and 'unspoken' (Reis, 2004) forms of dominance. Responsible senior executives may not even notice these forms of dominance because, as in Utopia, they are normal, naturalized and routine in life, such that it is not even worth discussing it. In Utopia, heterosexuality is differentiated by clothes, and the generational order of control passes through the male head of the family to other males. Children, wives and the elderly obey this natural order.

Although, in the global economy, we have societies and types of family arrangements where such a male-dominated natural order does not exist, heterosexual differentiation is still predominant, with the natural aim of maintaining the male order. Indeed, throughout Western history we have always had elite women who have transcended male organizations and/or generational orders (Baruch and Reis, 2015); however, this does not reflect any advance in the disappearance of gendered forms of patriarchy.

Regarding happiness, a critical perspective would promote reflection upon individual autonomy. Socially responsible executives could promote this individual reflection within their organizations with the support of independent professionals from the areas of psychology and sociology. As it was framed in Chapter 4 for leaders, it could be said that all individuals and employees would benefit from finding their self-actualizing tendencies in Rogers' (1959 and 1977) terms, and their imaginary perceptions/ misperceptions as under Lacan (1977, 1998 and 1991).

In Utopia people were allowed to learn as much as was necessary for the improvement of their minds because they were integrated in such collective social order in which they believed the happiness of their collective lives consisted. Nowadays, TM processes (knowledge to improve our minds) and organizations (an outlet for an order) have a big interplay of guiding individual careers and happiness.

References

Adler, P. S. & Kwon, S. W. (2002) Social capital: prospects for a new concept, *Academy of Management Review*, 27(1), 17–40.

Al Ariss, A., Cascio, W. F. & Jaap, P. (2014) Talent management: current theories and future research directions, *Journal of World Business*, 49, 173–179.

Aras, G. & Crowther, D. (2007) Sustainable corporate social responsibility and the value chain. In D. Crowther & M. M. Zain (Eds.), *New Perspectives on Corporate Social Responsibility*, Shah Alam, Malaysia: University Publication Centre, Universiti Teknologi MARA. 109–128.

Arthur, M. B., Inkson, D. & Pringle, J. (1999) *The New Careers: Individual Action & Economic Change*, London: Sage.

Arthur, M. B. & Rousseau, D. M. (1996) *The Boundaryless Career: A New Employment Principle for a New Organizational Era*. Oxford: Oxford University Press.

Baruch, Y. (2004) Transforming careers – from linear to multidirectional career paths: organizational and individual perspective, *Career Development International*, 9, 58–73.

Baruch, Y. & Reis, C. (2015) How global are boundaryless careers and how boundaryless are global careers? Challenges and a theoretical perspective, *Thunderbird International Business Review.* http://dx.doi.org/10.1002/tie.21712

Baruch, Y., Dickmann, M., Altman, Y. & Bournois, F. (2013) Exploring international work: types and dimensions of global careers, *International Journal of Human Resource Management*, 24, 2369–2393.

Bird, A. & Osland, J. (2004) Global competencies: an introduction. In H. W. Lane, M. L. Masnevski, M. E. Mendenhall & J. McNett (Eds.) *The Blackwell Handbook of Global Management: A Guide to Managing Complexity.* London: Blackwell. 57–80.

Borgatti, S. P. & R. Cross (2003) A relational view of information seeking and learning in social networks, *Management Science*, 49(4), 432–445.

Burt, R. S. (1992) *Structural Holes*, Boston, MA: Harvard University Press.

Campbell, J. L. (2007) Why would corporate behave in socially responsible ways? An institutional theory of corporate social responsibility, *Academy of Management Review*, 32, (3), 946–967.

Carroll, A. B. & Buchholtz, A. K. (2000) *Business and Society: Ethics and Stakeholder Management*. Cincinnati, OH: Southwestern Publishing.

Clarkson, M. B. E. (1995) A stakeholder framework for analyzing and evaluating corporate social performance, *The Academy of Management Review*, 20,(1), 92–117.

Crowther, D. & Aras, G. (2008) *Corporate Social Responsibility*, Frederiksberg, Denmark: BookBoon.

DeFillippi, R. J. & Arthur, M. B. (1994) The boundaryless career: a competency-based perspective, *Journal of Organizational Behavior*, 15(4), 307–324.

DeFillippi, R. J. & Arthur, M. B. (1996) *The Boundaryless Career*, New York: Oxford University Press.

Dickmann, M. & Baruch, Y. (2011) *Global Careers*. New York: Routledge.

Eby, L. T., M. Butts & A. Lockwood (2003) Predictors of success in the era of boundaryless careers, *Journal of Organizational Behavior*, 24(6), 689–708.

Fligstein, N. & Freeland, R. (1995) Theoretical and comparative perspectives on corporate organization, *Annual Review of Sociology*, 21–43.

Granovetter, M. (1973) The strength of weak ties, *American Journal of Sociology*, 78(6), 1360–1380.

Hall, D. T. (1976) *Careers in Organizations*, Pacific Palisades, CA: Goodyear Pub. Co.

Hall, P. A. & Soskice, D. (2001) An introduction to varieties of capitalism. In P. A. Hall & D. Soskice, *Varieties of Capitalism: The Institutional Foundations of Comparative Advantage*, Oxford: Oxford University Press. 50–51.

Hamori, M. & Koyuncu, B. (2011) Career advancement in large organizations in Europe and the United States. Do international assignments add value?, *International Journal of Human Resource Management*, 22(4), 843–862.

Ibarra, H. (2003) *Working Identity: Unconventional Strategies for Reinventing Your Career*. Boston, MA: Harvard University Press.

Inkson, K. & Arthur, M. (2001) How to be a successful career capitalist, *Organizational Dynamics*, 30(1), 48–58.

Jones, C. & DeFillippi, R. (1996) Back to the future in film: combining industry and self knowledge to meet the career challenges of the 21st century, *Academy of Management Executive*, 10(4), 89–104.

Jones, C. & Lichtenstein, B. (2000) The 'architecture' of careers: how career competencies reveal firm dominant logic in professional services. *Career Frontiers: New Conceptions of Working Lives*, 153–176.

Kakarika, M. 2009. External labor market strategy and career success: CEO careers in European and the United States, *Human Resource Management*, 48, 355–378.

Kirchmeyer, C. (2002) Gender differences in managerial careers: yesterday, today, and tomorrow, *Journal of Business Ethics*, 37(1), 5–24.

Kolko, G. (1963) *The Triumph of Conservativism*. New York: Free Press.

Koyuncu, B. (2011) Career advancement in large organizations in European and the United States: do international assignments add value?, *International Journal of Human Resource Management*, 22, 843–862.

Marcel, J. J. & Cowen, A. P. (2014) Cleaning house or jumping ship? Understanding board upheaval following financial fraud, *Strategic Management Journal*, 35(6), 926–937.

Margolis, J. D. & Walsh, J. P. (2003) Misery loves companies: rethinking social initiatives by business, *Administrative Science Quarterly*, 48(2), 268–305.

Marler, J., Barringer, M. W. & Milkovich, G. T. (2002) Boundaryless and traditional contingent employees: worlds apart, *Journal of Organizational Behavior*, 23, 425–453.

McCraw, T. (1984) *Prophets of Regulation*. Cambridge, MA: Harvard University Press.

Mitchell, R., Agle, B. R. & Wood, D. J. (1997) Toward a theory of stakeholder identification and salience: defining the principle of who and what really counts, *Academy of Management Review*, 22(4): 853–886.

Lacan, J. (1977) The function and field of speech and language in psychoanalysis. In *Écrits*. New York: Norton. 30–113.

Lacan, J. (1988) *The Seminars of Jacques Lacan Book II: The Ego in Freud's Theory and in the Technique of Psychoanalysis 1954–1955* (trans. S. Tomaselli). New York: Cambridge University Press.

Lacan, J. (1991) *The Seminars of Jacques Lacan Book I: Freud's Papers on Technique 1953–1954* (Trans. J. Forrester). New York: W. W. Norton & Co.

Langley M. (2013) Ballmer on Ballmer: his exit from Microsoft, *Wall Street Journal*, Nov. 17. Retrieved 5 October 2015, from http://online.wsj.com/news/articles/SB10001424052702303460004579194150724298162

Margolis, J. & Walsh, J. (2001) *People and profits?* Mahwah, NJ: Lawrence Erlbaum Associates.

Nahapiet, J. & Ghoshal, S. (1998) Social capital, intellectual capital, and the organizational advantage, *Academy of Management Review*, 23(2), 242–266.

Orlitsky, M., Schmidt, F. L. & Rynes, S. L. (2003) Corporate social and financial performance: a meta-analysis, *Organization Studies*, 24(3), 403–441.

Parker, H. & Arthur, M. B. (2000) Careers, organizing, and community. In M. A. Peiperl, M. B. Arthur, R. Coffee & T. Morris (Eds.), *Career Frontiers: New Conceptions of Working Lives*. Oxford: Oxford University Press. 99–122.

Peiperl, M. & Baruch, Y. (1997) Back to square zero: the post-corporate career, *Organizational Dynamics*, Spring, 7–22.

Peiperl, M. & Estrin, S. (2000) Chief executives in the New Europe: challenges, shortages, and an agenda for change. Brussels: Association for Executive Search Consultants (AESC) Europe.

Peirperl, M. & Jonsen, K. (2007) Global careers. In H. Gunz & M. Peiperl, *Handbook of Career Studies*. Thousand Oaks, CA: Sage. 350–372.

Raider, H. J. & Burt, R. S. (1996) Boundaryless careers and social capital. In M. B. Arthur & D. M. Rousseau, (1996) *The Boundaryless Career: A New Employment Principle for a New Organizational Era*. Oxford: Oxford University Press. 187–200.

Reis, C. (2004) *Men Working as Managers in a European Multinational Company*, München, Mering: Rainer Hampp Verlag.

Reis, C. (2010) Sensemaking of managers' ethical work orientations, *Social Responsibility Journal*, 6(1), 143–155.

Rogers, C. (1959) A theory of therapy, personality and interpersonal relationships as developed in the client-centered framework. In S. Koch (Ed.), *Psychology: A Study of a Science. Vol. 3: Formulations of the person and the social context*. New York: McGraw-Hill.

Rogers, C. (1977) *On Personal Power: Inner Strength and Its Revolutionary Impact*. New York: Delacorte Press.

Schein, E. (1996) Developments in the 21st century, *The Academy of Management Executive*, X(4), 80–88.

Schneiberg, M. (1999) Political and institutional conditions for governance by association: private order and price controls in American fire insurance. *Politics & Society*, 27(1), 67–103.

Segers, J., Inceoglu, I., Vloeberghs, D., Bartram, D. & Henderickx, E. (2008) Protean and boundaryless careers: a study on potential motivators, *Journal of Vocational Behavior*, 73(2), 212–230.

Sullivan, S. (1999) The changing nature of careers: a review and research agenda, *Journal of Management*, 25(3), 457–484.

Sullivan, S. E. & Baruch, Y. (2009) Advances in career theory and research: a critical review and agenda for future exploration, *Journal of Management*, 35(6), 1542–1571.

Thomas, D. C. & Osland, J. S. (2004) Mindful communications. In H. W. Lane, M. L. Masnevski, Mendenhall, M. E. & McNett, J. (Eds.), *The Blackwell Handbook of Global Management: A Guide to Managing Complexity*. London: Blackwell. 94–108.

Tymon, W. G., Stumpf, S. A. & Doh, J. P. (2010) Exploring talent management in India: the neglected role of intrinsic rewards, *Journal of World Business*, 45(2), 109–121.

Vaiman, V., Scullion, H. & Collings, D. (2012) Talent management decision making, *Management Decision*, 50(5), 925–941.

Valcour, P. M. & Tolbert, P. (2003) Gender, family and career in the era of boundarylessness: determinants and effects of intra- and inter-organizational mobility, *International Journal of Human Resource Management*, 14(5), 768–787.

Van Rooij, S. W. (2012) Training older workers: lessons learned, unlearned, and relearned from the field of instructional design, *Human Resource Management*, 51(2), 281–298.

Waddock, S. A. & Graves, S. B. (1997) The corporate social performance–financial performance link, *Strategic Management Journal*, 18, 303–319.

Wang, M., Adams, G. A., Beehr, T. A. & Shultz, K. S. (2009) Bridge employment and retirement: issues and opportunities during the latter part of one's career. In S. G. Baugh & S. E. Sullivan (Eds.), *Maintaining Energy, Focus and Options*

Over the Career: Research in Careers: Volume 1. Charlotte, NC: Information Age. 135–162.

Ward, A., Sonnenfeld, J. A. & Kimberly, J. R. (1995) In search of a kingdom: determinants of subsequent career outcomes for chief executives who are fired, *Human Resource Management*, 34(1), 117–139.

Weinstein, J. (1968) *The Corporate Ideal in the Liberal State*. Boston, MA: Beacon Press.

Index

Page numbers in **bold** refer to figures.

 Taylor & Francis eBooks

Helping you to choose the right eBooks for your Library

Add Routledge titles to your library's digital collection today. Taylor and Francis ebooks contains over 50,000 titles in the Humanities, Social Sciences, Behavioural Sciences, Built Environment and Law.

Choose from a range of subject packages or create your own!

Benefits for you
- » Free MARC records
- » COUNTER-compliant usage statistics
- » Flexible purchase and pricing options
- » All titles DRM-free.

 REQUEST YOUR **FREE** INSTITUTIONAL TRIAL TODAY

Free Trials Available
We offer free trials to qualifying academic, corporate and government customers.

Benefits for your user
- » Off-site, anytime access via Athens or referring URL
- » Print or copy pages or chapters
- » Full content search
- » Bookmark, highlight and annotate text
- » Access to thousands of pages of quality research at the click of a button.

eCollections – Choose from over 30 subject eCollections, including:

Archaeology	Language Learning
Architecture	Law
Asian Studies	Literature
Business & Management	Media & Communication
Classical Studies	Middle East Studies
Construction	Music
Creative & Media Arts	Philosophy
Criminology & Criminal Justice	Planning
Economics	Politics
Education	Psychology & Mental Health
Energy	Religion
Engineering	Security
English Language & Linguistics	Social Work
Environment & Sustainability	Sociology
Geography	Sport
Health Studies	Theatre & Performance
History	Tourism, Hospitality & Events

For more information, pricing enquiries or to order a free trial, please contact your local sales team:
www.tandfebooks.com/page/sales

 Routledge
Taylor & Francis Group

The home of
Routledge books

www.tandfebooks.com

For Product Safety Concerns and Information please contact our EU
representative GPSR@taylorandfrancis.com Taylor & Francis Verlag GmbH,
Kaufingerstraße 24, 80331 München, Germany

Printed and bound by CPI Group (UK) Ltd, Croydon, CR0 4YY
08/05/2025
01864440-0001